The Philosophy of Hinduism

FOUR SPANS OF HUMAN LIFE

Hindu Ashram Vyavāsthā

- Bhrahmacharya : The Foundation
- Grihastha : The Struggle
- Vanprastha : The Withdrawal
- Sanyasa : The Final Phase-Liberation

J.M. Mehta

Published by

Marketed by

Pustak Mahal®, Delhi

J-3/16 , Daryaganj, New Delhi-110002
☎ 23276539, 23272783, 23272784 • *Fax:* 011-23260518
E-mail: info@pustakmahal.com • *Website:* www.pustakmahal.com

Sales Centre

10-B, Netaji Subhash Marg, Daryaganj, New Delhi-110002
☎ 23268292, 23268293, 23279900 • *Fax:* 011-23280567

Branch Offices

Bengaluru: ☎ 22234025
E-mail: pustak@airtelmail.in • pustak@sancharnet.in
Mumbai: ☎ 22010941
E-mail: rapidex@bom5.vsnl.net.in
Patna: ☎ 3294193 • *Telefax:* 0612-2302719
E-mail: rapidexptn@rediffmail.com
Hyderabad: *Telefax:* 040-24737290
E-mail: pustakmahalhyd@yahoo.co.in

ISBN 978-81-223-1065-8

Edition : 2009

Printed at : Param Offsetters, Okhla, New Delhi-110020

The Philosophy of Hinduism

FOUR SPANS OF HUMAN LIFE

(Hindu Ashram Vyavāsthā)

Dedication

This book is dedicated to Swami Dayanand Saraswati – the founder of Arya Samaj. Most of the thoughts about Ashram Setup, contained herein are based upon views expressed by him, in his writings.

Contents

Preface

According to ancient Indian philosophy, human life has been divided into four parts or segments, and each such sub-division is known as an 'Ashram'. Before we discuss Ashram setup which constitutes 'Four Ashrams', it is necessary to understand the meaning of the word Ashram, which is derived from its Sanskrit root, *Shram* (श्रम). The meaning of 'Shram' is to get tired, to make efforts or to engage oneself in some hard work, etc. Thus the word 'Ashram' implies a place or field for hard work. Obviously, these four ashrams of Indian way of life are associated with some form of hard work in every situation or part of life.

In ancient Indian scriptures, there are prayers which express human desire for a life of one hundred years. Assuming that a normal person has a life span of one hundred years, the whole life has been divided into four equal segments or parts, each consisting of 25 years. This was the ancient original concept, however, in view of the changed circumstances and requirements, it may not be practisable to adhere strictly to this limit of time period and it may vary in each case. In present times, it is very rare that the life of an individual extends up to one hundred years. Therefore, at present, the life span cannot be divided into four segments of 25 years each. Particularly, in case of first two ashrams, the time limit of 25 years each, may not be possible. An individual may not be able to complete his education and acquire a profession within the time limit of 25 years. Again, a householder may also not be able to get his children educated and married and complete all his domestic obligations by the age of 50 years. Therefore, the time period of each ashram may have to be different in each case, depending upon the circumstances of an individual. But the division of life into four parts will remain.

The basic purpose of 'Ashram Setup' was to provide broad guidelines to all individuals on 'how to live life' in an orderly, well-planned and useful manner, going through different phases of life. Thus in each part of life, an individual was supposed to equip himself with necessary qualities and capabilities which would serve as efficient means to fulfill the requirements of that part of life, in an appropriate and purposeful manner. Naturally therefore, the first segment of life, which was considered as the most important, started with necessary training and preparation, which formed the basis for building the whole life structure and served as its strong foundation. Our Rishis called it *'Brahmacharya Ashram.'* It was followed by the next part in which a person got married, established a household, raised a family and fulfilled his worldly desires amidst pleasures and pains of existence. After living this period of life and going through its hardships, he reaches a stage when he realises that all the pleasures and comforts of life are of transitory nature and are mixed with pain. A desire, then, arises to get out of this hundrum of illusory life and with that yearning starts the next stage of withdrawal or disconnection from worldly life. This is the stage of transition from the life of a householder (called the *Grihastha Ashram*) to a life of detachment (called the *Vanprastha Ashram*), which continues for some years and is utilised as a period of preparation for the next and the final phase of life, known as *'Sanyas Ashram'*. In this final segment of life, one aspires to seek redemption or God-realisation, which is ordained in our scriptures as the final goal of human life. The process of life, as briefly outlined above constitutes 'Ashram Set up' and it forms one of the most important pillars of ancient Indian philosophy.

An attempt has been made in this small book to briefly explain this social setup, which is one of the most wonderful and beneficial contributions of Indian philosophy to the whole world for the welfare of all mankind. It is hoped that the general reader will greatly benefit from its contents.

J. M. Mehta
J-186 Saket
New Delhi

Ashram Setup
A Master Plan to Live Life

In order to uplift the quality of human life, the following verse in the Gita is most appropriate :

Udhareta ātmanā ātmanam,
na ātmānam avasārayate;
Ātmā yevahi ātmano bandhu,
ātmā yevam ripu ātmana.

ऊधरेत आत्मना आत्मानम, न आत्मानम अवसारयते।
आत्मा एवहि आत्मनो बंधु, आत्मा एवं रिपु आत्मन॥

[Verse 5, Chapter VI]

'Let a man lift himself by himself, let him not degrade himself; for the self alone is the friend of the self and the self alone is the enemy of the self.'

In the above verse, the Lord instructs us to uplift ourselves by our own efforts. There is no better means to do so, than the 'Ashram Setup' which occupies the most important place among all means to make our lives worthy, happy and noble.

Every normal individual in this world wishes to lead a good and happy life. Such a life has to be beneficial, successful, progressive and purposeful. Unfortunately, most human beings do not know how to achieve this objective. We make lots of mundane efforts without any success. The main reason for our failure is ignorance of the right means to attain the right goal.

In our real life, in general, the technique of good and happy living that should be noble and purposeful is neither taught at home nor at school or college and nor do we learn it from our own experience and environment. In order to achieve the desired goal, one has first to acquire the proper knowledge of the means to achieve it. In other words, the aspirant should have proper education, knowledge, suitable qualities, necessary training and discipline, besides actual application and practice of all that one has learnt and acquired.

Our education, in general, is subject and career oriented. It provides information on variety of topics and mainly serves as a base for a profession or career, so that one can earn a living. There is no sufficient scope for acquiring proper knowledge to lead a happy, holy and purposeful life. It is also not conducive to attain the true and real, final goal of human life. The subject matter being discussed in this book revolves around the right and organised way of living a purposeful life.

As Indians, we are fortunate to inherit the valuable legacy of wisdom and knowledge of our ancient Rishis and Sages (whom we may call as Spiritual Scientists). Those great thinkers and teachers, by virtue of their holy lives, deep thinking, analysis, and austere living (*Tapasya* or *Sadhna*), discovered and perfected the true way of right conduct, holy and happy living and designed a curriculum for living a worthy and noble human life. This way of living life is called 'Ashram Setup' (आश्रम व्यवस्था), which consists of four segments or stages of life, from birth to death. As a matter of fact, this is a 'Blueprint' or 'Master Plan' which lays down an ideal framework for living a good useful and purposeful life in all aspects.

What more can a human being wish for? In this small book, we shall try to deal with the four segments and stages of life, in the following chapters.

❑❑❑

Four Ashrams

A human being aspires to live around one hundred years. On the basis of this assumption and according to ancient Indian philosophy, human life has been divided into four stages or segments, each lasting around 25 years. This bifurcation of human life into four segments is called 'Ashram Setup' and each segment is called 'Ashram'. Thus there are four ashrams as follows :

1. *Brahmacharya.* This is a period for acquisition of knowledge under the supervision of a Guru (learned teacher) while residing with him.
2. *Grihastha.* This is a period of settled life in a house, after marriage.
3. *Vanprastha.* In this segment, one lives in a forest or away from home after fulfilling his domestic obligations.
4. *Sanyasa.* This is the last segment of life

when one leads a detached life and aspires for God-realisation.

Before we discuss each 'ashram' in some detail, it is necessary to know its meaning. The word *'Ashram'* is a Sanskrit word which is derived from *'Shram'*, meaning hard work. It also implies remaining engrossed, making efforts, restraint and *Tapasya,* etc. Thus, it is that part of life which involves hardwork. It is also a place or field where a disciple or a practitioner lives and performs hardwork.

In present times, an ashram is also considered as a place where monks, sadhus and other religiously inclined people or retired persons, who have discarded their homes or vice-versa, spend the remaining days of their life. Thus, there are ashrams for old people, for widows and for orphans, etc. Such ashrams are managed by some religious or sectarian organisations or by a holy person or by some guru or some similar individual or organisation. But the ashrams which fall under the 'Ashram Setup' do not come in this category.

An 'Ashram' for the purpose of this book is a segment or period of life involving hardwork, which has physical, moral and spiritual connotation. Its inter-alia includes performance of one duties, in accordance with the respective stage of life, religious studies, gaining of knowledge, meditation, practice of self-restraint etc. Briefly speaking, an ashram is that segment or period of life which relates to the foundation, struggle, (which means life of a householder), partial withdrawl from mundane life and the final phase of godly life. Thus, the four ashrams are spread over the entire gamut of life. Such a life has to be disciplined, based on restraint and moral rules. Whether this life is lived as a student, as a householder or a detached person, living away from homely comforts or as a recluse, who has relinquished the material attachments and its desires and temptations, *Shram* or hard labour remains an essential ingredient.

Our life is a journey from birth to death—from childhood to youth, middle age and the final phase, which culminates into death. People often forget about the finality of death, which should always be kept in mind. It does not mean that one should live in a fear of death which should actually be viewed as a gateway to another life. However, this does not also mean that one should try to live only for the sake of pleasure, simply because one has to die sooner or later and consequently, one must think only of enjoyments and pleasures of life before dying.

As said earlier, hardwork or labour (*Shram*) is an essential part of all segments of life. But hardwork has its fruits too. Thus, life is an intermix of labour and enjoyment of fruits of labour. Pleasure and pain are twin sisters.

In view of what has been briefly discussed above, we can conclude that the Ashram Setup provides a systematic and scientific plan for fulfillment of life through its four segments in which all aspects of life are taken care of. Undoubtedly, it is a Master Plan for living full life in an orderly manner: from creation to cremation. It covers the whole time-table of human existence in an efficient and judicious manner.

We shall now briefly describe each ashram in the following chapters, the consecutive order of different stages of life is as follows :

'Having completed his *Brahmacharya,* a man enters *Grihastha Ashram* (married life) and thereafter, *Vanprastha* and last of all becomes a *Sanyasi.*'

[Shatpath Brāhman]

❑❑❑

Brahmacharya Ashram

Meaning of Brahmacharya

In the 'Ashram Setup', the first segment of life, which spreads over initial twenty-five years, is termed as brahmacharya ashram. In order to understand the proper significance of this ashram, it is essential to comprehend the meaning of the word 'Brahmacharya.'

In common parlance, brahmacharya is generally considered as a period of celibacy. An unmarried person, who leads a life free from sexual indulgences is known as a *'brahmachari'* i.e. one who observes brahmacharya. But this is only a restricted definition of brahmacharya.

The word 'Brahmacharya' is composed of two parts *Brahman* and *Charya*. Brahma means God or the Supreme Power and Charya means conduct or the way of life, We may, therefore, conclude that the conduct, following which, one can attain

God or the Ultimate Reality is called 'brahmacharya'. It is therefore not mere observance of celibacy only but includes much more. Of course, observance of celibacy is one of the fundamentals of this ashram.

Who is a Brahmachari?

A simple answer to the above question follows from the meaning of the word 'Brahmacharya' as discussed briefly in the preceeding para. One, who observes brahmacharya in thought, words and deeds, is a *brahmanchari*. We will discuss this matter in greater detail as we proceed further. Let us see, what the great epic *'Mahabharat'* says in this context. It says:

"They alone who practise virtue, subjugate their passions and never lose their reproductive element, are true brahmacharis, and become learned men."

[Mahabharat Vidurniti]

The great sage 'Manu' lays down a very strict discipline for a *brahmachari*. It is given below.

'A brahmachari (male or female) should abstain from meat and alcohol, perfumes, garlands of flowers, tasty foods and drinks, the company of the opposite sex, sour articles and injury to all living beings; from anointing the body and handling the reproductive organ unnecessarily; from the use of books and shoes, and of an umbrella or a sunshade; from harbouring low passions such as anger, avarice, carnal passion, infatuation, fear, sorrow, jealousy and malice; from singing, dancing, playing, gambling, gossiping, lying and back-biting; from looking upon woman (with the eye of lust) and embracing them and from doing harm to other people and indulging in such evil habits. Let every student sleep alone and never lose his reproductive element. He who loses it through passion, breaks the vow of brahmacharya.'

The above is an extremely difficult and rigid discipline and it may be rather impossible for any one in the modern times to adhere fully to this regimen. However, any one following this discipline will surely lead a life of perfection.

Period of Brahmacharya

Normally, the period of first 25 years of life is termed as *'brahmacharya ashram.'*

For a student, Manu says :

"A student should observe brahmacharya and study the Vedas with their subsidiary subjets for 9, 18 or 36 years or until he has completely mastered them."

According to Manu, brahmacharya is of three grades:

(i) The Lowest : Man should be endowed with the most excellent qualities and in order to accomplish longevity, strength (physical and mental) and the like qualities, the shortest period for which a student should observe brahmacharya, is 24 years.

(ii) The Intermediate : The next grade of brahmacharya is for 44 years.

(iii) The Hightest : The highest grade of brahmacharya is for 48 years.

The period of brahmacharya may vary but the normal span is up to 25 years, after which one may enter the married life.

But *brahmacharya* has much wider implications also. For instance, one may remain brahmachari throughout life, from birth to death. Such a rare person may be called *'Bal Brahmachari'*. Some of the ancient Rishis had remained so. In recent times, Mahrishi Dayanand, the founder of Arya Samaj was one such person, who remained brahmachari throughout his life. Even other normal human beings who are inclined towards spirituality are expected to observe brahmacharya in other segments of life. The spirit of brahmacharya should prevail in all ashrams. Thus, a married man can also observe this discipline by practising self restraint in the matter of sexual indulgence. The sage Manu, on this subject, says :

'He who is contented with his own wife and avoids conjugal embrace on the eight forbidden nights *(ritugami)* is a *Brahmachari*, even though he may be a married man.'

Thus, a married man can also be a brahmachari by following the plan of generating a new life.

Similarly, a person who enters next two stages, viz vanprastha and sanyas has to observe brahmacharya. A person in vanprasth a ashram, abstain from sexual indulgence even when his own wife lives with him. In the last stage, a sanyasi has to renounce all connections with domestic life. For him the question of any sexual indulgence does not arise at all. In this way, the discipline of brahmacharya should be practised in all stages of life.

The Upbringing — Gurukul System

'मातृमान पितृमानाचार्यवान् पुरुषो वेद॥

[शतपथब्राह्मण ।]

Mātrimān Pitrimān Āchārayavān Purusho Veda.

[Shatpatha Brāhmana.]

'Verily, that man alone can become a great scholar who has had the advantage of three good teachers viz mother, father and teacher.'

Role of Parents

A mother is the first teacher of a child. Next in line comes the father and the teacher. The above verse shows the importance of three good teachers in the upbringing of a child. Blessed is the family and most fortunate is the child, whose parents are godly and learned. The healthy influence of a mother on her children surpasses that of any one else. No one else can equal a mother in her love for her children and in her anxiety for their welfare. Blessed is the mother, who never ceases to impart religious tone to the mind of her child from conception, till his knowledge attains perfection.

The role of both parents in the upbringing of the child is very important. It is a major factor in determining the future welfare of the child. A child's education and welfare starts well before the conception. First of all, they should follow the proper rules of sexual intercourse. Then, they have to be careful in the matter of diet, dress and personal conduct. Both parents before, during and after conception should avoid the use of harmful foods, such as intoxicating drinks, decomposed and non-nutritious food-stuff, prejudicial to the physical and intellectual growth of the child. They should make use of those articles which promote health, strength, energy, intellect and good temper. They should practise abstinence and take all necessary precautions so that they beget children of high mental calibre, strength and energy.

As the children grow up, the mother should instruct them in a suitable manner, in order to make them healthy and refined in character and mannerisms. Parents should make all efforts to inculcate in the minds of their children, an intense desire for knowledge, good company and control of the senses. Thus, the elementary foundation of the personality of a *brahmachari* has to be laid during childhood.

It is during childhood that parents and teachers should see and try to enforce that the children should avoid useless and harmful playing, unnecessary crying, laughing and wrangling. The children should not be allowed to indulge in excess of pleasures and sorrows, eating and other useless pursuits, which produce jealousy, malice, hatred, greed, anger, etc. A proper check should be maintained over their sexual instincts and inclinations. In no case they should be allowed to handle or rule their reproductive organs, in order to avoid any loss of reproductive element. In short, the parents should try in every possible manner to inculcate such sterling qualities in their children, as fearlessness, truth, patience, body resistence, cheerfulness, peace, good temper and respect for their elders.

Gurukul System

According to ancient system of education, the mother should instuct the child from birth to the 5th year and the father from the 6th to the 8th. In the beginning of the 9th year, the child should be sent to school called *'Acharyakul'* or *'Gurukul'* where the teachers were supposed to be learned and thorough scholars, imbued with a sense of piety and great responsibility, well-versed in various sciences. They were masters of their subjects and men of great character. Boys and girls were sent to separate schools (Gurukuls), which were located far away from towns and cities, in forest area. The teachers and other workers in boy's schools were all males and in girl's schools all females. The boy's schools were located at least 3 miles away from girl's schools. The students were called 'brahmacharis' and they were required to abstain from the following eight kinds of sexual excitements vis-a-vis persons of opposite sex :

1. Looking upon them with lust.
2. Embracing.
3. Having sexual intercourse.
4. Playing with them.
5. Associating with them.
6. Reading or talking about amorous and sexual matters.
7. Intimately conversing with them.
8. Indulging in lustful thoughts and activities.

The Principles Underlying the Gurukul system

A detailed discussion on the Gurukul System of education is beyond the scope of this small book. However, some general principles underlying this system are stated in the following page :

1. The teachers should make all efforts to ensure that the students (brahmacharis) keep aloof from all sorts of sexual excitements, as the preservation of the vital fluid is one of the fundamentals of brahmacharya ashram.
2. During their stay in the gurukul, the students are expected to perfect their knowledge, cultivate amiable habits and manners, gain in strength of the body and mind and thus develop into a healthy and happy youth before they enter married life.
3. The gurukul should be, at least, 5 miles away from a town or a village.
4. All the students must be treated alike in the matter of facilities, e.g. food, dress, accommodation, etc. without any distinction of social status.
5. All students, be they princes or commoners should practise strict physical and mental discipline as prescribed in the gurukul.
6. They should not be allowed to hold any communication with their parents.
7. They should be freed from all worldly or domestic worries and anxieties and thus should devote themselves wholly to their studies.

8. The teachers should accompany their students in all their activities so that they do not indulge in any mischief or misconduct or become lazy.
9. The brahmacharis should not solicit bodily comfort. They should bear all sorts of hardships.
10. They should fully devote themselves to the acquisition of knowledge, culture, etc.
11. 'Simple living and high thinking' should be the motto of their life in the gurukul.

The Scheme of Studies in a Gurukul

A brief outline of the scheme of studies under the ancient gurukul system is stated as follows :

1. First of all comes Phonetics. It was the duty of parents to teach their children, at home, to pronounce different letters. The greater knowledge of proper phonetics was imparted to them, while they lived in the gurukul.
2. Then they were taught Grammar, which involved detailed study of roots of words, groups, prefixes, suffixes, etc. The complete science of grammar was mastered in 3 years when students became acquainted with the construction of all words of general Sanskrit literature. With the proper knowledge of the science

of grammar, the learning of other sciences became easy.

3. The knowledge of Vedic vocabulary and philology came next.
4. The above was followed by the teaching of prosody, which enabled the students to master thoroughly the rules of Vedic and Sanskrit verification.
5. The students were then taught *'Manusmriti'*, *'Valmiki Ramayana'*, the *'Vidurniti'* and some other selections from the Mahabharata. The study of these books inculcated in the sudents good habits, eradicated evil tendencies and made them refined and cultured.
6. Six schools of philosophy (six *Darshans*) were then taught, with the expositions of Rishis who were enlightened great souls. The students also studied ten *'Upanishadas'*. All these courses were finished in 2 years.
7. Therefater, the students studied the Four *Vedas,* with their four *Brahmans*, with proper accent and meanings. This took a period of six years.
8. After the study of Vedas, the students were taught *Upvedas,* which are four in number, as follows :
   i. ***Ayurveda* (Science of Health) :** This included works of great Rishis,

Charak and Sushrut and other sages, who were experts in medical sciences. This course of studies included medicine, therapeutics, physiology and pathology, hygiene and dietetics, climatology and the sciences of temperaments, anatomy and surgery with the proper use of instruments etc. in a period of four years.

ii. ***Dhanur Veda*** **(Science of Governence) :** It consists of two parts, as follows :

(a) Civil Part : It included the art of governing, protecting lives and property of the people, developing economy of the country, right administration of justice and making the people happy and contented by proper and just governance, etc.

(b) Military Part : It comprises organisation of the army, use of fire arms and knowledge of different types of drills, tactics and strategy, etc.

iii. ***Gandharva Veda*** **(Science of Music)** : This includes study of different parts of music, singing, playing of instruments, dancing, etc.

iv. ***Artha Veda*** **:** This is science of mechanical arts, also known as *Shilpa Vidya*. It involves study of laws of matter and motions and making of various types of machines, etc. In short, this study provides knowledge of nature and properties of all substances. This science helps in increasing the wealth and prosperity of a country.

9. Thereafter, the students learnt *Jyotish Shastra,* which included Arithmetic, Algebra, Geometry, Geography, Geology and Astronomy.

It is not possible for us to describe as to how the above scheme of studies were actually practised and what were the elaborate courses of instruction. It is also not clear to us that how many subjects were taught in various ashrams. May be different subjects were taught in separate ashrams. However, it can be assumed that a brahmachari, on completion of 24-25 years and after completing his education in an ashram, should leave the portals of a *gurukul* as a strong, healthy young man of good moral conduct, fully capable to enter the life of a householder. After completing his education in the gurukul, he would get married and enter into a profession to earn his livelihood and establish a household.

General Approach to Observance of Brahmacharya

Broadly speaking, there are two essential aspects in the observance of brahmacharya. These are: complete abstention from sexual indulgence and preservation of the vital fluid (semen). But this is a restricted view, as brahmachaya has a much wider meaning, which involves complete control of all senses through mind, senses and actions. It is a matter of self-restraint versus self-indulgence in all aspects of life. Besides sexual organs, control has to be exercised over senses of sight, speech, touch, task and actions. It must be kept in mind that brahmacharya does not merely mean celibacy.

While observance of brahmacharya involves complete self control over all the senses, the control over the sexual urge remains the vital part of this discipline. It is said that the victory over the sexual instinct is the greatest victory. There is great stress on the preservation of the vital fluid as it is essential to maintain physical and mental health. It becomes a shield against hardships of life and also provides immunity against diseases. In exercising self-control, the control must be in thought, speech and action. If the thought process gets out of control, the other two are adversely affected.

As observance of brahmacharya involves purity of body and mind; simple living and strict discipline, some special rules and regulations are required to be followed by a brahmachari. Some of these are briefly stated below :

1. **Non-violence :** This means absence of hatred, enmity and bad feelings towards all beings.
2. **Truth :** One must practise truth in all possible manner in thought, speech and action. Try to know truth, then have faith in it and then speak and write which is true.
3. **Non-stealing :** One should not take, steal or possess something on which one has no right.
4. Complete abstention from sexual indulgance in thought, word and deed.
5. **Non-greed :** It means one should not acquire or possess more than what is necessary for simple living.

The above rules constitute a social code of conduct, which must be practised by a brahmachari for his own good as well as for the welfare of the society in which he lives. Besides these rules, a brahmachari has also to observe the following rules of personal conduct :

1. *Cleanliness.* One must maintain both external and internal cleanliness. While external cleanleness is maintaned through water and wearing clean clothes, etc. and by keeping the environment clean, internal purity is observed by practising moral and spiritual conduct.

2. *Contentment*. One should remain satisfied with his lot after making full efforts according to his capability and capacity.

3. *Tapa (Penance)*. This is the practice and attitude to face all difficulties and hardships of life without grumbling and maintaining calm and patience.

4. *Swadhyaya (Study of good literature)*. It involves study of scriptures and other good literature, which promotes moral values and good conduct and makes life worthy and truly happy.

5. *Ishwar Pranidhan*. This involves full faith and devotion to the Supreme. One must live in the awareness of God's presence and perform all actions accordingly.

The above rules are known as *Yamas* and *Niyamas* and form part of Mahrishi Patanjali's *Ashtang Yoga*. We have mentioned these rules very briefly here.*

Helpful Aids for Observance of Brahmacharya

After understanding the basic concept of brahamacharya and also knowing its main rules (*Yamas* and *Niyamas*), it is essential to know and practise the means to achieve it. While it may be easy to know and memorise the theory part of

---

* For their detailed description, the reader may like to read the book entitled 'Essence of Maharishi Patanjali's Ashtang Yoga' by the author and published by 'Pustak Mahal, Darya Ganj, New Delhi.'

the discipline, the major difficulty arises in its actual implementation, which is very difficult indeed. For the proper observance of brahmacharya, one may find recourse in some helpful aids, some of which may be mentioned below.

1. Proper Food. Food plays an important role in the observance of brahmacharya as it influences the functioning of both—body and mind. To follow this strict discipline, the control of the palate is absolutely essential. Food should be simple, wholesome, natural and nourishing. One must not be a slave to the taste. One should not eat just to please the palate but to keep the body and the mind going and in good health. One must not simply live to eat but eat to live a simple, healthy life. In short, a *'Satvik'* food will serve as a useful aid for the proper observance of brahmacharya. Such a food should not be stale, harsh and hot and must not excite the eater for sensual pleasures. It should promote well-being, strengh, joy and cheerfulness and has to be soft, sweet, nourishing and agreeable. Alcohol, meat, drugs and all other intoxicants must be avoided. Good *satvik* food helps in mind control and through it, the sexual instinct. It must be, therefore, kept in mind that food plays an important role in the observance of brahmacharya.

2. Good Thoughts. The observance of brahmacharya becomes easy if one inculcates good, positive and pure thoughts. It is necessary to disapprove, discard and curb sensual desires, as soon as these arise in the mind. It is the mind which is the seat of all desires. It is therefore, absolutely essential, to control the mind by practising self restraint through the control and training of the sense organs. While some external constraints may be helpful, brahmacharya is not simply a virtue, which can be cultivated by external constraints only or by forced suppression. Its observance involves proper understanding of its role and significance in shaping life and achieving its goal. This is possible only through appropriate, well-regulated efforts of the will to control the wayward mind. Such a control has to be in thought, word and deed.

The practice of 'auto suggestion' will serve as a helpful tool in the observance of brahmacharya. One should constantly feed his mind with following suggestion. 'Brahmacharya gives strength to my body, peace to my mind and happiness to my spirit. It gives brightness to my intelligence and will lead to a healthy, happy and long life. Therefore, it is my prime duty to observe and preserve brahmacharya.' Thoughts like these will help in the observance of brahmacharya while thoughts of sexual pleasure and indulgence will disturb and obstruct the practice of brahmacharya.

3. Exercise. Physical and mental exercise help in the observance of brahmacharya. Exercise helps in the proper digestion and assimilation of vital essence, produced by the bio-chemical process of eating food. It utilises vital energy and promotes good health. Mind can be kept engaged in useful activities through physical and mental exercise. Walking and yogic asanas are good means of physical exercise, while reading, writing and cultivating some hobby are beneficial forms of mental exercise. Taking part in outdoor sports and indoor games is another means of useful exercise. Execise keeps one busy in desirable pursuits and therefore promotes positive and productive thinking. There is a saying 'an idle mind is a devil's workshop.' Exercise, therefore, is useful in the production, conservation and proper utilisation of vital energy and thus helps in the proper observance of brahmacharya.

4. Meditation and Prayer. Prayer and meditation channelise the thinking process towards the worship of God, who is the source of purity, goodness and bliss. Brahmacharya, basically, is a process of self-control, which is not possible without constant devotion to God. Prayer and meditation are essential means for this process as these activities act as safeguards against evil thoughts and nefarious designs and actions. Regular prayer and meditation promote full faith in God with a spirit of devotion and self-surrender and thus save a person from falling a prey to worldly temptations, which include sensual pleasures of life. Prayer and meditation, therefore, are effective means for the observance of brahmacharya.

5. Study of Good Literature. Reading of good healthy literature helps in the observance of brahmacharya. Good reading provides a healthy and useful direction to thoughts, which lead to action. It is said, 'Thought is father to the deed.' Before performing an act, first the thought arises in the mind and that thought prompts an action. Good thoughts, therefore, produce good actions. In the observance of brahmacharya, thought control is of paramount importance. Study of good literature which should include books on religion, philosophy, arts & sciences, etc. can play a vital role in the cultivation of good, healthy, pure and useful thoughts. Good reading can strengthen the resolve to maintain and keep up the desire to cultivate and practise the strict discipline. Thus literature, which contains thoughts for self-improvement, acts as a useful aid to the observance of brahmacharya. One must, therefore, avoid bad company, sensual literature and other media means, such as erotic films, videos, etc., which arouse sexual thoughts and excite enjoyment of sensual pleasures leading to sexual indulgence and loss of vital fluid.

Apart from special rules and useful aids for the observance of brahmacharya mentioned above and earlier, I shall now mention some tips and suggestions for daily practice and these must be followed on regular basis in every day life. These will be found useful in the proper observance of brahmacharya on short and long-term basis. Some of these may be briefly stated, as follows :

1. Do not eat without natural hunger and eat less than your capacity at each meal.
2. Avoid non-vegetarian, fried food with excess ghee or oil, heavy sweets and preparations containing excess of spices.
3. Avoid alcohol and other intoxicating drinks and habit forming beverages which include tea, coffee and colas, etc.
4. Do not take food items and snacks which are heavy on the stomach and difficult to digest.
5. Dinner should be light and should be taken a couple of hours before sleeping.
6. Follow the saying, 'Early to bed and early to rise, makes a man healthy, wealthy and wise.'
7. Treat female conpanions like sister or mother, according to the age and never cast lustful glances on women folk.
8. Never try to be alone in female company, as far as possible.
9. Always try to remain occupied physically and mentally. It is admirable to cultivate some useful hobby or good reading habit.

10. Avoid bad company, unproductive immoral gossip, amorous literature and such films, etc.
11. Remembrance of God's name, recitation of some short holy mantra is always helpful.
12. Follow any other helpful suggestion, exercise or activity, which you may find useful from your personal experience.

The main objective of adopting above and similar other suggestions, means and measures is to inculcate the spirit of brahmacharya so that when one crosses the threshold of the first segment of life, one is fully equipped with good health, proper education, professional skill, besides moral values and is thus fully prepared to enter the next segment of life, which is *'Grihastha Ashram'* or the life of a householder and married person.

It may be pertinent to mention here, that the observance of brahmacharya does not culminate in the completion of the duration of brahmacharya ashram. This is the first stage of life in which the discipline of brahmacharya has to be observed in toto. However, the spirit of the same discipline has to be maintained and continued throughout life, although it may be less rigid, as one passes through the successive three ashrams. It should be kept in mind that the final goal of life is God-realisation, which is not possible without the proper observance of the spirit of brahmacharya in thought, word and deed, during all segments of life.

The Importance of Brahmacharya

Brahmacharya is the mainspring of all other ashrams. It lays the foundation of life. It is during this period that a brahmachari would acquire knowledge, under the guidance of a learned guru while living in a gurukul, away from the worldly environments, evils and temptations. Living an unmarried life, he would protect his vital fluid and grow into a healthy youth, following rules of nutrition and good health. By virtue of brahmacharya, vital forces called *Vasus* are fully developed and matured. These help to produce the noblest qualities in the body, mind and the spirit. Thus, a full grown brahmachari is a fully developed person in all the three aspects of human life *i.e.* physical, mental and spiritual. Thus, brahmacharya becomes means of all, that is best and the source of all, that is good and noble in life.

The importance of brahmacharya lies in the benefits which accrue from its proper observance. Some of these benefits may be briefly mentioned as follows :

1. The first benefit is that the observance of brahmacharya leads to concentration of mind and self-control, which are sure means to happiness.

2. The second benefit is that a brahmachari gets the light of knowledge which removes darkness of ignorance, and the true knowledge is source of all happiness.
3. Observance of celibacy preserves vital fluid and leads to good physical and mental health. A brahmachari leads a disease free long life.
4. By following special rules (*Yamas* and *Niyamas*) a brahmachari acquires moral values and social virtues, which make him a noble individual.
5. Equipped with physical strength, moral values and spiritual inclinations, a brahmachari is blessed with fearlessness, forbearance and fortitude which are invaluable assets of human life.

All these acquisitions, gained through the period of brahmacharya, in the healthy and noble environment of an ideal gurukul, would produce an ideal individul-fit in all respects to enter the portal of *Grihastha Ashram*.

The following *shloka* indicates the importance of brahmacharya in a few words as follows :

Brahmacharyena tapasā devāh
mrityumupādyanat

ब्रह्मचर्येण तपसा देवाः मृत्युमुपाघ्नत्

'It implies that by means of brahmacharya and the force of spiritual and physical hardwork, the learned can conquer even death!'

It is natural that one who has knowledge and physical strength is without any fear, even that of inevitable death.

In conclusion, it may be said that brahmacharya lays the firm foundation of entire human life and it is a stepping stone to a happy, healthy and ideal married life.

Special Features of Brahmacharya Ashram

In ashram setup, each ashram is different and has its own pecularities, although these are all inter-connected and one ashram leads to another. Brahmacharya ashram which covers the first phase of life (up to 25 years) has its following special features:

Celibacy. A brahmachari remains unmarried up to a minimum period of 25 years and he is supposed to be free from sexual indulgence during this period. In order to practise the extremely difficult discipline in thought, word and deed, one has first to know and fully understand the meaning and conditions of observing brahmacharya. We have already discussed these aspects in the chapter of 'Brahmacharya Ashram'.

Good Health. A brahmachari is supposed to enjoy the best of physical and mental health which follows from the complete observance of celibacy, besides proper food and excercise. He keeps busy in the daily routine and has no time for idle, negative thoughts which are harmful to health. He possesses a robust physique and is free from any disease and deformity.

Education. This is the period when a brahmachari acquires knowlede of all sorts under the supervision of a learned guru. At this segment of life, the foundation of proper education is laid down which is essential in all aspects of life. Thus on the completion of brahmacharya, one is fully equipped with various types of knowledge and qualities, which enables him to meet the challenges in subsequent periods of life. Complete proper education is therefore an important and special feature of this ashram.

Simple Hard Life. Brahmacharya ashram constitutes a period of simple and hard life. The student gets up early in the morning and is kept busy throughout the day in the performance of his daily duties, which include personal hygiene, regular studies, service to the guru, all odd jobs for the maintenance of the ashram. These daily chores not only keep him busy throughout the day, but also gives him enough excercise to keep in good health and nurture good thoughts, as well. By virtue of simple regular hard life, he acquires moral values, physical strength and positive thinking — all of which enable him to develop into an ideal youth.

Some Important Views on Brahmacharya

Mahatma Gandhi : In recent times, Mahatma Gandhi was one of the greatest votaries of brahmacharya. Some of his views on this subject may be quoted as follows:

'Brahmacharya literally means that mode of life which leads to the realisation of God. That realisation is impossible without practising self-restraint. Self-restraint means restraint of all the senses. But ordinarily, brahmacharya is understood to mean control over the sexual organs and sexual instinct. This becomes natural for the man, who exercises restraint all round.

The absence of seminal discharge is a straight forward restult of brahmacharya, but it is not all. There is something very striking about a full-fledged brahmachari. His speech, his thought and his actions, all bespeak possession of vital force.

So long as the desire of intercourse is there, one cannot be said to have attained brahmacharya. Only he who has burnt away the sexual desire in its entirety, may be said to have attained control over his sexual organ. Such a brahmachari does not flee from the company of women. For him, the distinction between men and women almost disappears.

And maintenance of perfect health, should be considered almost an utter impossibility without brahmacharya, leading to the conservation of the sexual secretions.

A married couple is worthy of being considered brahmachari if they never think of sexual intercourse, except for the purpose of procreation. Such an intercourse is not possible unless both parties desire it. It will never be resorted to in order to satisfy passion without the desire for a child.

'What is brahmacharya? It is the way of life that leads to Brahma — God. It includes full control over the process of reproduction. The control must be in thought, word and deed. If the thought is not under control, the other two have no value...' Brahmacharya is such, only if it persists under all conditions and in the face of every possible temptation.

Brahmacharya is not a virtue that can be cultivated only by outward constraints. The true brahmachari will shun false restraints. But the aspirant, undoubtely, needs them, even as a young mango plant has need of a strong fence around it.

As an external aid to brahmacharya, fasting is as necessary as selection and restriction in diet. So overpowering are the senses that they can be kept under control only when they are completely hedged on all sides, from above and beneath. It is a common knowledge that we are powerless without food and so fasting undertaken with a view to control the senses is, I have no doubt, very helpful.

Sex urge is a fine and noble thing. There is nothing to be ashamed of it. But it is meant only for the act of creation. Any other use of it, is a sin against God, and humanity.

The world seems to be running after things of transitory value. It has no time for the others. And yet, when one thinks a little deeper, it becomes clear that it is the eternal things that count in the end...one such thing is Brahmacharya."

The views of Gandhi Ji, as briefly mentioned above, indicate the great significance of brahmacharya in human life. He took the vow of brahmacharya in 1906 and kept it till his death. Such was his resolve and firm faith in the observance of this strict and essential discipline of self-restraint. He had written extensively about brahmacharya, its importance and benefits in his several writings, but it is not possible for us to include more in this small book. The reader will surely benefit from what has been briefly stated above.

Atharva Veda

The following *shloka* of Atharva Veda shows the importance of brahmacharya :

Brahmacharyena tāpasā devāh mrityumupādyanat.

ब्रह्मचर्येण तपसा देवाः मृत्युमपाघ्नत् ।

'The learned through the strict discipline of brahmacharya can keep death away.'

Such is the power of brahmacharya.

Patanjali Maharishi

According to *Yoga Darshan* of Maharishi Patanjali, who is the founder of Yoga, brahmacharya is one of the five *Yamas* of Ashtang Yoga as stated in the following *shloka* :

Ahimsā, satya, asteya, brahmacharya, aparigrah, yamāh.

अहिंसा, सत्य, अस्तेय, ब्रह्मचर्य, अपरिग्रह यमाः

Ahimsa, truth, non-greed, brahmacharya, non-acquisition are five *Yamas*.

Brahmacharya pratisthāyām veerya lābhah.

ब्रह्मचर्य प्रतिष्ठायां वीर्य लाभः

The observance of brahmacharya leads to the preservation of vital fluid, which is the source of immense strength.

The Bhagwad Gita

In verse 11, of chapter 8 of the Gita, the importance of the brahmacharya is stated as follows :

Yadichchhanto brahmacharya charanti.

'यदिच्छन्तो ब्रह्मचर्य चरिन्त'

Those who aspire for the highest goal of life practise brahmacharya.

Gautam Buddha

In his *Dhammapada,* Gautam Buddha says:

Acharitvā brahmachariyam
alddhā yobbane dhanam;
Senti chāpātikhānā
wa purānāni anutyunam.

अचरित्वा ब्रह्मचरियं अल्द्धा योब्बने धनम्।
सेन्ति चापातिखाणा व पुराणानि अनुत्युनम्॥

Those who do not practise brahmacharya, do not earn wealth while young and those who repeat their past mistakes, they lie down like an old broken pot.

In another place, he says, 'indulgence and disease are companions and brahmacharya is the basis of freedom from disease'.

Chhandogya Upnishad

According to this upnishad, a true brahmachari does not suffer from any discomfort and pain.

Yagyavalkya Rishi

A *shloka* in the Yagyavalkya treatise says,

Manasā vāchā karmanā
sarvāvasthāsu sarvadāh;
Sarvartra maithun tyāgo
brahmachāri pravaksheta.

मनसा वाचा कर्मणा सर्वावस्थासु सर्वदा!
सर्वत्र मैथुन त्यागो ब्रह्मचारी प्रवक्षेता॥

Preservation of vital fluid through mind, word and deed, in all circumstances always is termed as complete brahmacharya.

Manu Smriti

According to an edict in Manu Smriti, a brahmachari should sleep alone and should not waste his vital fluid. Any willful wastage of vital fluid destroys the vow of brahmacharya.

Shankaracharya

According to Shankaracharya, 'brahmacharya is the highest austerity. One who has attained brahmacharya has achieved the status of a god.'

Sant Tulsi Das

With full confidence and responsibility, sant Tulsidas says,

'The observance of truth, humility and brahmacharya lead to God-realisation'.

Maharishi Dayanand

The observation of the great Rishi is as follows:

'Brahmacharya includes complete restraint over sexual indulgence. Those who conserve vital energy, they are free from disease and achieve four objectives of *dharma, Artha, Kama* and *Moksha*.'

Mahavir Swami

This is how Mahavir instructed his followers to observe brahmacharya:

Dharmārāme chared bhikshu
dhritimān dharma sariyah
Dharmarāma rato dāntah
brahmacharya samāhitah.

धर्मारामे चरेद् भिक्षु, धृतिमान धर्म सारियः।
धर्मराम रतो दान्तः ब्रह्मचर्य समाहितः॥

'A disciple with perseverence, who rides on the vehicle of true religion (*Dharma*), engaged in its comfort controls his senses, must practise and observe brahmacharya.'

Swami Vivekananda

He stressed the importance of conservation of vital fluid, in order to acquire and maintain the power of memory and concentration of mind. This will help in studies.

Vinoba Bhave

He was the greatest devotee of Mahatma Gandhi. He advocated practice of brahmacharya for both men and women. According to him, the goal of brahmacharya is to devote one's life in search of God and to attain God-realisation. He recommended observance of this discipline for the achievement of higher goals of life including social service etc.

Mahatma Anand Swami

Brahmacharya includes remembrance of God at all times and preservation of vital fluid by practising self-restraint.

In the foregoing pages, an attempt has been made to describe brahmacharya in its various aspects. In conclusion, this ashram, which covers the first segment of life, is the most important of all ashrams. This is because, it lays down the very foundation of human life and it is the vital period for the preparation of subsequent segments. Full control of mind and senses, observance of complete celibacy, physical and mental fitness, acquisition of proper knowledge and skills are the many ingredients of upbringing in this ashram, which is the most important period of life. The observance of complete celibacy in mind, word and deed makes this ashram the most difficult of all ashrams. Keeping in view its utmost importance, this most precious period of life should not be wasted in mundane pleasure seeking pursuits. The complete observance of brahmacharya is therefore essential in letter and spirit.

❑❑❑

Grihastha Ashram

After completing brahmacharya ashram, a brahmachari is fully prepared to enter the next phase or segment which is the married life of a householder. This ashram is termed as Grihastha Ashram. The meaning of *grihastha* is located in a house. In this segment, an individual gets married, raises his family, lives in a house with his parents or establishes a separate household. Since he has to maintain his family and run a household, he must, therefore, acquire a profession in order to earn his living. It may be trade, agriculture, some service or any other job which provides means of livelihood, depending upon his education and skills, which he had acquired during the first ashram.

Who is a Grihastha?

An individual, who after completion of brahmacharya ashram, gets married, establishes a fixed abode and lives with his family, is called a *grihastha*. It is natural that in order to lead the life of a householder such a person must follow a profession to earn his livelihood. He can be a teacher, a trader, an agriculturist or an official of the state or may follow some other profession according to his skills and capacity. It is pertinent to mention here that, this is the only ashram in which an individual lives in a house of his own at a particular place, with the members of his family. The position is different in case of other ashrams. A Brahmchari lives in a guru's ashram under his supervision, a Vanprasthi would live far away from his established residence, in a forest or some other remote area, while a Sanyasi is not supposed to maintain a permanent residence, as he is required to keep on moving from one place to another, except for a short period during the rainy season.

Some Ancient Thoughts on Marriage

The great Rishi Manu has expressed thoughts on marriage, some of which are quoted below:

'Let a brahmachari who has not violated his vow of brahmacharya and has conducted himself righteously according to the advice of his preceptor, enter married life after the completion of his studies'.

'A girl who is not descended on his mother's side within sixth degree (generations) and does not bear the same family name (gotra) as his father's, is eligible for marriage.'

The marriage among near relatives is not considered desirable as it results in the deterioration of the off-spring. Similarly, marriage in families which are irreligious and devoid of character and those suffering from certain diseases, which can be transmitted to the offspring, is also not recommended. In short, both husband and wife should come from good (physically, morally and intellectually) families.

The best time for marriage for a girl, is from sixteenth to the twenty-fourth year of her life and for a man, from the twenty-fifth to the forty-eighth year. The marriage of a girl of sixteen with a man of twenty five is considered inferior. Of a girl of eighteen or twenty with a man of thirty-five or forty is considered of medium quality. The marriage between a girl of twenty-four with a man of forty-eight is called superior marriage.

The best form of marriage is by choice after the completion of the education of the contracting parties, besides, proper observance of brahmacharya by both sides. Brahmacharya and perfection of knowledge are the basis of true happiness in married life. It is best that the marriage should be under the control of the contracting parties. In case parents are arranging a match, it should be done with the consent of both the parties. The real factors in marriage are the bride and the bridegroom and not their parents. It is they, who will be happy if they agree well together and only they will suffer miserably, if they disagree. According to Manu, the secret of a happy marriage is as follows:

"In whatsoever family, the husband is content with his wife and the wife with her husband, it is there and there only that happiness, wealth and honour dwell permanently."

The marriage by choice (*Swaymvara*), which is considered the most ancient form of marriage, is the best. Before a man and a woman think of marrying, they should see that they suit each other in point of knowledge, human nature, character, age, beauty, strength and family background, etc.

According to Rigveda, 'men of quick perception and action, energetic, in full youth, strong in body, and capable of discharging reproductive functions should marry maidens, who are young, dear to them, and enjoy long life, blessed with children and grand children. Both men and woman should practise brahmacharya, acquire knowledge, perfect their character, gain in strength of body and soul and attain full youth before getting married'.

Pain and Pleasure in Grihastha Ashram

Grihastha ashram, nowadays, is generally considered more a period of struggle and strife, and less a source of pleasure. For most of us, who lead a married life, there seems to be more unpleasant experiences than the pleasant ones. The period of pleasure lasts only for a short period of honeymoon and some more thereafter. The problems start with birth-pains and they continue to linger on with the rearing and bringing up of children. The running of the household brings a lot of challenges and hardships. The bringing up of children, their healthcare and education, fulfillment of mundane desires and meeting the household requirements, professional cares and other allied responsibilities put considerable strain on the married couple. The problems get enhanced if both husband and wife are working and there is no one else to look after the needs of the household. In the competitive, hurried and stressful life of modern times which brings forth unlimited desires, a problem is cropping up at every step. On top of it, there are ever increasing demands of unfulfilled cravings of the material world which put lots of burden on the economic resources of a household. All these factors and a few more make *grihastha* a cauldron of unpleasant experience.

Originally, *grihastha* was not meant to be so. Life is a long, hard journey involving different stages. To start with, brahmacharya ashram involved strict discipline and hard work. After the completion of the first difficult phase of life, *grihastha* was envisaged to provide a stage of comfort and enjoyment on the turbulent path of life long journey. In order to make the lifelong journey easier and pleasant, the provision of a helpful marriage partner was included in the ashram set-up. The mutual attraction between man and woman was supposed to form the basis of a healthy and happy married life. A happy and healthy loving couple can lay down the foundation of a happy, purposeful and fruitful domestic life. Husband and wife have been compared to two wheels of a vehicle. This shows the equal importance and utility of both man and woman for the successful management of a household. A woman's role is no less important than that of man's for a happy family life. Rather, a woman plays greater and more important role than a man, as she has to perform several roles, which include those of a wife, a companion, a mother and a daughter-in-law, etc. It is said that 'a woman can do what a man cannot do.' The main responsibility of child birth and early rearing-up and feeding the infant lies on her. It is she who runs the major share in the gamut of house management and its daily chores.

It is an acknowledged fact, that *grihastha ashram* has a pivotal role to play in human life.

It is therefore essential, that its incumbents should possess some special qualifications, in order to make this period of life a very pleasant experience. The main qualifications are being mentioned below:

(*i*) Good Health — Both husband and wife should be physically and mentally fit, strong and active

(*ii*) They should practise moral values and inculcate virtues of righteousness.

(*iii*) They should be broad-minded, loving, accommodating and cooperative.

(*iv*) They should be optimist, cheerful and have a positive attitude to life and its activities.

The above list is not exhaustive and more qualities can be added in the light of individual experience. In the absence of these qualities, the married life is likely to be more troublesome and painful. An individual who has these qualities will easily earn his livelihood and will never be short of wealth and prosperity. He will have a healthy and happy family and shall also be able to make a useful contribution to the society and the country.

It is mentioned in the scriptures, that a *grihastha* seeks companionship of a woman in marriage, for living a happy and comfortable life. At the time of marriage, both husband and wife exchange vows of mutual cooperation and trust and to remain faithful to each other. It is ordained that the married couple should perform their domestic and social duties with willing cooperation and joint understanding, keeping moral values and remembrance of God in all their ventures. Thus, *grihastha ashram* is a joint family venture to live worldly life happily and also to practise good moral conduct in such a manner, that a happy and beneficial future life (after death) is also ensured.

In short, while *grihastha ashram* has its pain and pleasure both intermixed, depending upon how it is planned and actually lived, it can be full of worldly comforts and pleasures, if it is lived in a planned, purposeful and orderly manner. It becomes painful and full of pitfalls if it is lived as an uncontrolled, pleasure seeking exercise, full of harmful excuses and selfish desires. Self-control and self-restraint are main pillars of a happy and healthy grihastha ashram. One is free to exercise one's own option and face the consequences of pleasure and pain as the case may be.

Main Causes of Misery in Grihastha Ashram

In the present times, for most householders, grihastha ashram has become full of misery and misfortunes. They generally attribute this to fate or effect of past *karmas*. While *Karmas* do play their role, there are causes of our own making, some of which are stated below:

1. Unsuitable Marriages — This is one of the major causes of unhappiness in a *grihastha*.

Marriages are not being arranged in accordance with rules and regulations laid down in the scriptures. As marriage form the very basis of a healthy and happy married life, it should be solemnised keeping in view the age, family background, personal traits, physical and mental fitness and the intrinsic nature of both the partners. It should not be arranged merely on the basis of physical beauty, sexual attraction or greed for wealth. In many cases, the last two factors become the sole criteria for marriage and most of such marriages fail in the long run. Consequently, a marriage which is supposed to be a source of conjugal and perfect human relationship, becomes rather a curse. As a result of such unsuitable and unhappy marriages, the number of suicides and unnatural deaths happen quite often these days. Persons of opposite qualities and nature should never enter into a wedlock.

2. Unequal Social Status and Disrespect for Women — Unequal social status of women and a general attitude of apathy and disrespect for women folk, especially in rural areas, is another cause of pain and misery in *grihastha jeevan*. In a male-dominated society, women in our country had remained suppressed and kept illiterate and were made to occupy on inferior position in the society. How could there be happiness and prosperity in a household if one partner, who has a major role in the running of a household, is kept suppressed and in a miserable condition? In some remote corners, the women were treated as virtual slaves and even sold like a commercial commodity. The undesirable practice of *Sati* in some areas is another example of female degradation. Even today, in spite of advancement in education and respect for human rights, the birth of a girl child in the family is considered a curse rather than a happy event, especially in rural backward areas. Sometimes, even natural parents and other male members adopt an attitude of disdain and discrimination towards the female inmates of the family. Such a situation of social inequality does not augur well for happy household. However, there is a ray of hope with the spread of female education, and conditions are looking better with the awakening in society.

3. Absence of Mutual Tolerance — This is another major cause of sour family relations in *grihastha ashram,* where tolerance is essential to maintain and sustain natural furlongs of love, proper understanding, friendliness and unity within the household. Social family bickerings and disputes originate from the absence of tolerance among family members. First of all, both husband and wife must practise the attitude of tolerance with each other. They should set an example for others in the family. Children learn fast by example than by precept. In an ideal situation, no family member should utter an insulting, hateful or disparaging remark against another family member. However, such occassions arise when one is in haste or in anger, some member of the family says something undesirable, unpleasant or displeasing against someone else in the family. In such circumstances, there is instant need to practise tolerance to diffuse the ill effects created earlier by wrong utterance. Any point of difference, discord or friction in family relations should be discussed mutually in a cool and peaceful atmosphere and solution can be found amicably. If necessary, guidance and assistance can be sought from elders, family well-wishers, friends and relations. In all such cases of discord, the practice of tolerance is the right and ultimate solution.

4. Individual Selfishness and Personal Ego — An attitude of utter selfishness and personal ego are also largely responsible for unhappiness and dissatisfaction in family relations. If husband exhibits superiority and gives precedence to his personal needs and requirements over those of his wife and other members of the family, it creates bad feelings and a sense of jealousy among others, who feel neglected and ignored. In this way, selfish attitude and egoism play a dominant role in relationships between husband and wife, mother-in-law and daughter-in-law, parents and young children and even brothers and sisters, etc. This dangerous disease of selfish conduct has broken several homes and has destroyed peace and harmony existing in numerous families. This is also one of the major causes of divorce among married couples. When such an attitude is rampant in the society at large, it results in the disruption and disintegration of the whole social set-up and norms of social behaviour. On a broader scale, it can become the main cause of disharmony among religious sects and conflict among nations leading to wars and mass destruction. Proper care and precautions are, therefore, needed at the level of every household so that this evil is nipped in the bud and the disease does not acquire an epidemic form.

5. Excessive Sex Indulgence — This is another cause of misery in *grihastha ashram.* While it may be admitted that sexual instinct is natural to mankind, and *grihastha ashram* provides an excellent forum for its indulgence, yet it is essential to observe proper limits. It could be kept in mind that marriage does not offer an unlimited license to fulfill sexual desire, which has no end. Unlimited sexual indulgence can cause havoc to the health of a married couple as well as their offspring. Craving for the satisfaction of carnal desire can also lead to dangerous and incurable diseases like HIV, etc. Sexual instinct, therefore, has to be kept within proper restraint, in the interest of healthy and happy domestic life. According to scriptures, sexual acts should be performed only for procreation but this is an ideal which is extremely difficult to achieve. In such circumstances, self restraint, to the extent possible, is the practical way to maintain happy and enjoyable family life.

Marriage is a social and legal bond between husband and wife and it should be considered sacred and lifelong. Any sexual relation outside marriage is taboo and within marriage it has to be kept within desirable limit. One must always remember that self-restraint is the essential safeguard against self-indulgence.

Means of Happiness in Grihastha Ashram

In the preceding paras, we have described briefly the causes of misery and unhappiness in the *grihastha ashram*. It is said that pleasure and pain go side by side. Human life is a mixture of joy and sorrow and *grihastha ashram* is the playground for both. We shall now make an attempt to describe some of the major means of happiness in this ashram.

All householders want happiness in their family life. The main object of married life was supposed to make an entry into a life of comfort and happiness. At the time of entering into wedlock, our marriage rituals lay stress on this aspect and the married couples also undertake and exchange vows to make each other happy and comfortable. The *grihastha ashram* is meant to fulfill common desires, such as acquisition of wealth and property, having children, earning name and fame and to make all sorts of material progress in order to enrich life with peace, pleasure and prosperity. But all these acquisitions and pleasures of life have to be kept within reasonable and desirable limits as excess of everything, even comforts and pleasures, is bad. As desires are insatiable, these must be kept within proper limits, otherwise unlimited fulfillment of mundane desires can lead to harmful consequences.

In order to make *grihastha* a happy and purposeful *ashram*, it is necessary to make suitable efforts for achieving the desirable end. Some of the means which may be adopted to cultivate happiness in this **ashram** are briefly mentioned below.

1. Good Conduct — Both husband and wife should speak and act in a loving and respectful manner. One must show due regard for the feelings and sensitivity of the other person. General behaviour should be based on mutual love, respect and proper understanding. Both should act in a manner, which is exemplary and would result in the welfare of the family as a whole. One should not think only for oneself but actually work for the comfort and happiness of all the inmates of the household. The motto should be 'Married life is a joint venture for mutual happiness.'

All inmates of a household should act in a manner which is deserving of a good human being. The fundamental role of good conduct lies in a *shloka* quoted below:

Ātmanah pratkulāni paresh na samācharet

आत्मनः प्रतिकूलानि परेश न समाचरेत्

[Mahabharata]

'Whatever act you don't consider good for you is not good for others too'

There is also an English saying: '.......... On to others as you wish to be done by.'

If you expect love and respect from others, you have to first love and respect them.

No member of the family should act in a disgusting, disgraceful and disrespectful manner. All conduct should be based on love, mutual respect, fellow feeling and keeping in mind the welfare of one another and the entire family.

2. Even Mind — The life in *grihasta ashram* is a combination of opposite situations: pleasure and pain, joy and sorrow, victory and defeat, honour and dishonour. Such opposite situations arise throughout life. In these situations, a householder generally adopts different attitude. One is likely to get overjoyed and overexcited in a pleasing situation, such as: marriage, birth of a child, winning of a lottery, etc. Again one is full of sorrow in case of an unpleasant situation like death, disease, failure in an examination, etc. The reaction in both cases is undesirable and may cause unhappiness. In a pleasant situation, there is no obligation to be over excited and no cause for despair in an unpleasant event.

The solution lies in being even minded in all situations. In the performance of all actions in life the following *shloka* from the GITA, shows the way :

Karmanya wādhikāraste mā
phaleshu kadāchanah;
Mā karmaphala hetuh bhurmā
sango astrah akarmani.

कर्मण्यवाधिकारस्ते मा फलेशु कदाचनः।
मा कर्मफलहेतुः भूर्मा संगोऽस्त्वकर्मणि॥

It means that one has right to action but not over its fruit. One should act without concern for its fruit but there should be no attachment to inaction. Thus, all actions have to be performed without worrying unnecessarily for their consequences which may be accepted with even mind, whatever the case may be. With this attitude, one will not get disheartened even when the result of one's action is not according to the expectation.

Life will then move on smoothly. This is positive thinking and the right way to face even the difficult situations in *grihastha jeevan*.

Cheerfulness

There should be an environment of cheerfulness in the household. Such an environment can make a home, a veritable heaven and its absence hell. A homely cheerful welcome by a housewife can erase the gloom and depression of a tired husband who returns home in the evening or at night after a full day's hard work. Similarly, a husband returning home from work need not burden his wife and family with a sad commentary on the cares, concerns, nasty happenings and experiences at work place. Small children at home, their playful pranks and smiling faces can lit up even gloomy environment and mood of any at home. Children need not be scolded for their small naughty tricks and childish acts. Both husband and wife should try to maintain an atmosphere of cheerfulness and this will promote cheerfulness in the children, as well. Every person has virtues and defects both and both partners should be fully conscious of their good and bad habits. One should try to bring improvements in each other's behaviour through pleasant discussion and interaction, without negative and undesirable criticism and without uncalled for fault finding. It is essential to keep smiling, as far as possible, in order to spread happiness in the family.

Spiritual Domestic Environment

Human life is a combination of body, mind and spirit. Life would be happy if all the three ingredients are kept in harmony. In order to make life harmonious and happy, the body should be kept healthy, the mind under control and the spirit in peace.

While wealth and material accessories are essential for a comfortable and happy domestic life, control and peace of mind and real happiness are not possible without proper spiritual environment. A rich man, with all his wealth and material possessions, may still feel miserable and unhappy if he has no peace of mind. Wealth can provide material comforts but not real and lasting happiness. For real, genuine and lasting happiness, one has to turn his attention towards God who is the source of permanent bliss. In order to make *grihastha ashram* full of happiness, it is essential to make it God-oriented for which suitable spiritual environment is essential. For this, one has to practise Dharma or true religion and not just perform only rites and rituals. Present and social conduct must be based on the practice of moral rules and spiritual practices, which include daily prayer, meditation, reading of good healthy literatures, and company of good, pious people. Purity of thoughts and personal conduct are essential for the creation of spiritual environment in the household. Elders in the family must set healthy practices and examples for the youngers to emulate. Spiritual environment brings inmates of a household closer to God and away from evil thoughts, deeds and tendencies and thus keep misery and unhappiness far away.

Some people have formed a wrong impression that it is neither necessary nor possible to maintain a spiritual environment in a *grihastha*, as it is meant for only *vanprastha* or *sanyasa ashrams*. Such thinking is completely baseless and is the brain wave of only the ignorant and pleasure-seeking people. Some of the great Indian rishis, saints and religious guides were *grihasthis*. We have examples of Lord Rama, Krishna, Sant Kabir, Tulsidas and many others. Guru Nanak and other Sikh gurus had their household. Infact, *grihastha* is the testing ground for sustaining an atmosphere in which spiritual growth and progress can be made possible in the face of all sorts of temptations and obstacles.

Loving Attitude

An attitude of love among the members of the family lays down the very foundation of a happy *grihastha jeevan*. A loving relationship among the members of the household binds them as a magnet binds iron filings. Such relationship has to be cultivated without any selfish motive, without any thought of individual gain or loss and without any expectation in return. Such is the love of mother for her new born, or the love of a young sister for her young brother when she ties the Rakhi thread around his wrist. An attitude of pure love involves sacrifice. One has to ignore personal gain or comfort or other similar benefit for the sake of others whom one loves. Such an attitude of love depends upon absence of any pride or prejudices, ego or selfishness. It is something inborn, natural and voluntary. Mutual respect, sweet conversation, helpful nature, proper understanding of a situation and fulfilment of each others' needs — all these factors help in the creation of a loving environment in the household. All mutual distrust, misunderstandings, conflicts and complaints must be removed as soon as these arise. It is said 'nip the evil in the bud.' If these small precautions are taken care of, there will be no cause for misery. Where love and mutual affection prevail, happiness follows and grihastha ashram becomes a haven of happiness.

Economy in Expenditure

Domestic income, expenditure and savings play a significant role in the maintenance of a happy household. Domestic expenditure, in no case, should exceed the income. Follow the saying 'cut your coat according to your cloth'. Control of expenditure, by and large, depends upon the wise and economic handling of a married couple. The responsibility of keeping the domestic expenditure within proper limit mainly depends upon the housewife. Family requirements of food, clothing and other necessary household material must be kept within reasonable limit and in any case, well within income resources. Money should be spent in a judicious manner, only on essential personal and household requirements. Unnecessary expenditure, just for ostentation or mere show of wealth, is uncalled for. All avoidable expenditure, on costly clothing and other household items, need not be incurred. A spendthrift wife or husband are likely to become pauper and thus be the cause of destruction of domestic peace and happiness. They will also spoil their children. Unlimited fulfillment of mundane desires and greed can lead to undesirable and harmful consequences, including debt, litigation and poverty. Some money should always he saved for the rainy days, while some suitable allowance should also be made for deserving charitable causes and general public welfare.

Some families incur unnecessary and avoidable expenditure on costly clothing, jewellery, furniture, means of transport, social events, etc., just to show off their rich status. Similarly unnecessary expenditure is also incurred on smoking, drinking, gambling, eating out in costly hotels. This is undesirable and a lot of money can be saved and properly utilised elsewhere, by not indulging in wasteful expenditures. It is, therefore, not only desirable but also essential to exercise economy in all spheres of personal, household and social expenditure. In any case, expenditure should be foreseen, properly planned and kept within one's income and capacity.

If one has money in excess, part of it should be invested in secure saving schemes for future needs and unexpected exigencies like sickness and medical requirements, etc. Part of it may be utilised for providing financial and medical assistance to the deserving needy, underprivileged, disabled poor people, etc. It will not only give them relief but will also be a source of personal satisfaction and happiness.

In conclusion, the householder should keep his desires and expenditure within the desirable and reasonable limits. All money should be utilised properly for meeting genuine essential needs of the household. In no case, any money should be wasted. This is the key to the economic prosperity and happiness of *grihastha ashram*.

Role of Man and Woman in Grihastha Ashram

Both man and woman are equal partners in married life. They are compared with two wheels of a carriage, sharing the burden equally. The carriage will not move smoothly if one wheel is damaged. Therefore, both husband and wife have to share equally the responsibilities and benefits of married life. Both should have mutual respect, pleasing in nature, accommodating and quite content with each other.

If the wife does not love and please her husband, being unhappy, he will not be sexually excited and consequently, no offspring will be produced. Even if children are born, they will be of inferior type.

If the husband does not please his wife, she being unhappy, the whole family will he unhappy and miserable. If both husband and wife are quite contended, the whole family will enjoy happiness and prosperity.

Husband and wife are the two main pillars of the edifice of Grihastha Ashram. About the role of a woman, the great *Rishi Manu* says :

"Let a woman attend to her household work most cheerfully and with great dexterity, keep her utensils and apparel clean, her house tidy, her furniture free from dust, all eatables pure and clean. Let she never lavish in expenditure. Let her cooking be done so nicely that the food may act on the system like a good medicine and keep away diseases. Let her keep a proper account of her expenditure and show it to her husband, use her servants properly and see that nothing goes wrong in the house."

About the role of man, Manu says:

"Let a man utter what is true and say what is pleasing. Let him not speak a disagreeable truth. (e.g. Let him ever call a one eyed man, one eyed) Nor let him speak an agreeable falsehood. This is the true conduct of life. Let him speak gently and kindly and avoid altercation and enmity with any." The woman should be treated with respect. In this context, Manu says:

"Let woman always be honoured by their fathers, brothers, by their husbands and the brothers of their husbands. They all should speak sweetly to the women and provide them with good food, new clothes and ornaments and keep them happy. Those who seek prosperity and happiness should never inflict pain an women."

"Where women are honoured, in that family great men are born, but where they are not honoured, all acts become fruitless. Where women pass their days in misery and sorrow because of the misdeeds of their husbands, that family soon perishes, but where they are happy because of the conduct of their husbands, the family continually prospers."

The above narration shows the great importance of the roles of man and woman in *grihastha ashram*. Thus, both should perform the true conduct of life in their respective roles as briefly stated above and consequently bring happiness and prosperity to their household.

Five Mahayajnas *Or* Five Great Daily Duties

A *grihastha* should perform five *mahayajnas* (daily duties) to the best of his capacity and ability. These mahayajnas (or five great daily duties) are briefly described below:

1. ***Brahma Yajna :*** It comprises studying and teaching the holy scriptures (Vedas and other holy literature), morning and evening devotion and practice of yoga discipline. It consists of following three parts:

a. ***Stuti*** **(Glorification of God) :** God is formless, invisible, all pervading and kept in mind. One must try to understand various attributes, functions and nature of God and make all efforts to mould one's character and conduct in consonance with the concept of God.

b. ***Prarthna*** **(Prayer) :** One should pray to God and express gratitude and seek His blessings. He should seek God's help after making all possible efforts for a desirable cause or want. Prayer should be genuine, from the heart and moral in nature.

c. **Upasana (Communion) :** It means coming close to God. It involves deep concentration, purity of mind, full faith and devotion. Self control and complete detachment from the external world are necessary. *Pranayam* and remembrance of God's name with proper understanding and complete devotion are helpful in this process.

2. *DEVA YAJNA* : It involves *Agnihotra* (*Homa*) which comprises the feeding of fire with *ghee* (clarified butter) and other purifying herbs, while reciting mantras from the holy scriptures (Vedas). It includes advancement of knowledge by association with the learned and the good and by cultivation of purity, truthfulness and similar other noble qualities. The *Homa* substances (such as ghee, musk, camphor, saffron and other herbs) used in *Agnihotra* keep the air pure and promote health, strength and intellect.

The above two *yajnas* (*Brahma Yajna* and *Deva Yajna*) should be performed daily, during morning at sunrise and in the evening at sunset.

Pollution is becoming one of the biggest health hazards of the modern world. Man is the biggest producer of pollution because of many enterprises which include factories, industries, motor vehicle and several other means of modern day life, which have become major pollution producing agents. The gases and smoke produced by these sources are polluting the space every moment. Man himself is a small factory of pollution. He wishes to inhale fresh air, drink fresh water and eat fresh food but exhales bad air, spreads foul smells and dirt. *Yajna* has been described as the noblest action and a means to heaven, as may be noticed from the following Sanskrit quotations:

Swarga kāmo yajeta.

स्वर्गकामो यजेत!

Those who aspire for heaven, should perform *Yajna*.

Yagyo wai shreshtam karma

यज्ञो वै श्रेष्ठतमं कर्म.
यज्ञ श्रेष्ठतम कर्म है.

(Brahman Granth)

There are other shlokas too in holy scriptures, which convey a definite message that *Yajna* is a sure means to peace, happiness and purity of physical and mental environment. The sacred mantras which are recited at *Agnihotra*, if properly understood and actually practised in daily life, shall produce healthy vibrations, positive impressions and will make life purposeful and productive at the personal and social levels. The thoughts expressed through these mantras can purify and improve human conduct and lay the very foundation of healthy society.

3. Pitriyajna : It consists in serving the learned, great teachers, scholars, parents, old people, great men, great yogis, and holy persons. This *Yajna* is divided into following two parts:

i. *Shraddha* : This word is derived from *Shra* which means truth. That by which truth is accepted and practised is called *Shraddha*. Thus, that which is done with *shraddha* i.e., with the object of embracing truth is called *shraddha*.

ii. The second part of this yajna is *Tarpana* which means anything done to one's parents, and other elders (who are alive) and make them happy. Tarpana is divided into following three parts:

A. *Brahma Tarpana* : The learned men and women should be respected, honoured and served properly ... to make them happy.

B. *Rishi Tarpana* : It consists in serving and honouring great teachers, their pupils, companions and assistants.

C. *Pitri Tarpana* : It consists in thoroughly satisfying *Pitrs*, by offering them most regularly food, clothes, conveyance, etc. In other words, it consists in offering them full service by doing everything in one's capacity, to keep their bodies healthy and their souls happy. The *Pitrs* include parents, grand parents, learned people who promote knowledge of physical and other sciences, who administer justice, who promote health and happiness, who provide security and protection and those who further the cause of truth and righteousness.

It should he borne in mind that *Pitriyajna* is meant for the living persons and not for the dead.

The practice of offering oblations to the dead parents, grand parents, etc., is wrong and undesirable and this arises out of ignorance.

4. *Vaishwadeva Yajna* : It involves offering of some part of cooked food to fire in the kitchen. Such food should be sweet other than sour and saltish, and its purpose is to spread sweet smell and purify the air in the kitchen. Some food should be placed on the ground in front of the house for dogs, insects, etc., or placed on the roof for birds such as crows, etc. Some food should also be given to the hungry outside or other people who are in distress and suffer from disease or disability and thus cannot earn their living.

The purpose of this *Yajna* is to purify the kitchen air and to offer help to creatures, other animals like stray dogs, etc. and to those who are distressed and need food.

5. *Atithi Yajna* : An atithi is one who comes unexpectedly and whose date of coming is not fixed or certain. In ancient days, a *SANYASI* who is virtuous, scholar and preacher of truth and righteousness used to move around preaching for the good of all, would visit householder, unannounced without any prior knowledge of the *grihastha.* It was the duty of the householder to offer him water, make him comfortable and give him food and other things, such as clothes, etc.

and thus serve him and make him quite at case. The *Sanyasi* used to impart proper knowledge and offer him advice for good and righteous conduct and help him in acquiring virtue and other desirable possessions. The *grihastha* should ensure that he is serving and honouring only a genuine *Sanyasi* and not an unholy, selfish, fraudulent individual in the garb of a religious person.

The above five *mahayajnas* should be practised by a *grihastha* as part of his daily duties. Some of the benefits of these *yajnas* are briefly mentioned below:

1. *Brahmayajna* : The performance of this yajna leads to advancement of knowledge, refinement of character, righteousness and brings one close to God. It makes the life of the performer virtuous, peaceful and happy.

2. *Agnihotra* (Homa) : On Collective basis, when most of the householder perform the *yajna*, it results in the purification of air, timely rain and is conducive to universal welfare and happiness. Purification of air, water and environment promotes good health, energy and sound intellect. This *yajna* is called Devyajna, as it purifies Devas like air, water, food, etc.

3. *Pitri Yajna* : The service of one's parents leads to a happy, healthy and peaceful household life, which promotes knowledge and wisdom. Since our parents served us in childhood and brought us up, it is our essential duty to serve them in return in a spirit of gratitude.

4. *Vaishwadeva Yajna* : It causes purification of the kitchen air. It helps us discharge our obligations towards the sick, the helpless, the needy including birds and animals who are dependent on us for sustenance. It is also in the nature of atonement for the pain and suffering, which we unknowingly inflict on the lower creation, in the daily routine of our lives.

5. *Atithi Yajna* : The service to the genuine and learned *atithis,* such as sanyasi of the highest order who move around from place to place and spread knowledge and moral values, is one of the great social obligations of a householder. It leads to universal progress and happiness. The householder can also attain spiritual knowledge while sitting at home and this brings improvement in his personal and social life.

Judging from the benefits which accrue from the performance of five *Mahayajnas*, it should to obligatory for a householder to perform them as part of his daily duties, according to his power and capacity. The performance of these *yajnas* will no doubt bring progress and improvement in the life of an individual, but it will no doubt, produce all round happiness in the society at large and the whole universe, as well.

Some Special Features of Grihastha Ashram

After conducting a detailed discussion on the various aspects of *grihastha ashram,* we may summarise below some of its special features, which may serve as a ready-reckoner for the reader.

1. Marriage : Marriage is the special feature which forms the base of this ashram. On the completion of the *brahmacharya ashram,* an individual is fully fit and prepared to enter into married life. The main purpose of marriage is procreation. The period of manhood lasts between 25-40 yrs. and this is the right time to get married. Marriage is a pure bond between husband and wife and it is their duty to produce and nurture noble off spring. It may be kept in mind that the institution of marriage is not a free license for pleasure seeking pursuits through unlimited sexual indulgence, which should be properly regulated through self-control.

2. Fulfilment of Desires : Grihastha ashram covers the prime period of youth in life. It is the period which is full of desires and aspirations which relate to sex, profession, wealth, name and fame and other material aspects. A person gets married and fulfills his desire for sex and children. He follows some profession and acquires wealth. He builds a house, raises his family and establishes a household and thus leads a comfortable life. It is, therefore, in this ashram that one gets ample opportunities to fulfil all mundane desires, which can not be fulfilled in any other ashram.

Social Contribution : A *grihastha* does not lead an individual isolated life. He is one unit of the whole society in which he lives and interacts. As a teacher, trader, doctor or businessman, he makes his individual contribution for the welfare of the society, community and the country. In this way, he not only earns wealth, but name and fame also, besides serving his country. All great men, leaders, thinkers, professionalists, social workers, freedom fighters etc. were mainly from *grihastha ashram*. It is this ashram whose inmates make moral and material contribution to support the people in other ashram. This is, therefore, a great social contribution from *grihastha ashram*. In fact, the main material progress of the society depends upon the social contribution made by the people of *grihastha ashram*.

Fixed Abode : It is only in *grihastha ashram* that one establishes his own fixed residence. A *brahmachari* lives in a 'gurukul', a *vanprasthi* lives in a forest and a *sanyasi* has no fixed residence at all, as he roams from place to place. This is, therefore, a special feature of this ashram only.

Some Important Views On Grihastha Ashram

Each ashram has its own utility and importance, according to the role it plays in human life.

However, grihastha ashram is considered the backbone of the ashram setup, in view of its pivotal role in the social structure and its peculiarities. According to Maharishi Manu, grihastha ashram is the greatest among all ashram on the basis of great responsibility it carries on its shoulders. Some of the important views, expressed by great men, on grihastha ashram are quoted below.

Maharishi Manu

This is what he says in Manusmriti

Yathā nadi nadāh sarve
sāgar yānti sansthitim;
Tathā shraminah sarve
grihastha yānti sansthitim.

यथा नदी नदाः सर्वे सागर यान्ति संस्थितिम् ।
तथा श्रमिणः सर्वे गृहस्थ यान्ति संस्थितिम॥

As all rivers, great and small, finally find their abode in the ocean, in the same way, all other ashrams find their support in the *grihastha ashram*. He further says that as all living being get their sustenance from air, in the same way, all ashrams owe their existence to *grihastha ashram*.

Another verse in Manusmriti depicts the greatness of this ashram, as follows:

The *grihastha ashram* is the greatest among all ashrams, because it is only the grihastha that provides food and other necessities of life to the people of other three ashrams (*Brahmacharya, Vanprastha* and *Sanyasa*).

It is observed that the responsibility of nurturing and sustaining other ashrams lies with *grihastha ashram*. All other ashrams depend on grihastha ashram for their food and other resources. A *brahmachari* and a *sanyasi* would go to a village for their food. Similarly, householders would supply food and other requirements of *vanprasthi,* who would live in a nearby forest area. Even now, where followers of other ashram reside are supported by householders through financial and material means. All the existing *'gurukuls'*, where *brahmacharis* live and study, the *vanprastha ashram* and other ashrams, where retired persons and others who have renounced their households go and live are mostly run on the basis of donations made by householders. Consequently, the grihastha has become the main support and the resource base of all other ashrams and hence it is of great importance.

Maharishi Dayanand

The great rishi, who was the founder of the Arya Samaj, has also indicated the great importance of grihastha ashram, in the following words:

'In the absence of this ashram, there would have been no procreation and consequently the existence of other ashrams would not have been possible. This is the ashram in which all desires which include physical comforts, material wealth, fame, family and children, get fulfilled.'

It may therefore be well said as the 'Mother of all ashrams.'

Valmiki Ramayana

The following *shloka* in Valmiki Ramayana is noteworthy:

Chaturnām āshramānāncha garhasthyam shreshtham uttamam;
Yatha mātah amāshritya sarve jivanti jantwah.

चतुर्णामाश्रमाणाञ्च गार्हस्थ्यं श्रेठमुत्तमम् ।
यथामातरमाश्रित्य सर्वे जीवन्ति जन्तवः॥

Rishi Valmiki says:

'Among all four ashrams, grihastha is the greatest. As all living beings live comfortably under the patronage of mother, in the same way all inmates live comfortably in *grihastha ashram*.'

Yajur Veda

According to Yajur Veda, there is no need to be afraid in *grihastha ashram*.

Taittariya Brāhmin

According to this *brāhmm granth, grihastha ashram* provides an opportunity to an individual to pay off his paternal debt. This is done by marrying and producing noble offspring, which is allowed only in *grihastha ashram*.

The above views on *grihastha ashram* may not be complete. There may be several other similar views expressed by other great men.

It is evident from the above discussion that *grihastha ashram* occupies the prime place in human life. It is not only important for an individual but also for the whole society. Grihastha is the middle part and the main battleground for the battle of life. It is the period when an individual passes through the maximum variety of experiences of actual living and these include – panic and pleasure, name and fame, comfort and discomfort, victory and defeat, honour and shame, loss and gain, fulfillment of desires, and other ups and downs of life. These experiences provide great opportunity in the development and progress of human personality.

It may be concluded that the progress of human civilisation depends upon *grihastha ashram*. Most of the work force required for the administration of a country and production of its material is provided by the inmates of this ashram. All organisations, industry, agriculture, educational institutions and other economic and social set-ups are run mainly by *grihasthas*. The vast majority of work force in various sectors of society comes from this ashram. It is difficult to run any functional agency without the support of *grihastha ashram*. In a nutshell, this ashram is the backbone of society and consequently, the greatest of all ashrams.

❑❑❑

Vanprastha Ashram

Having completed his brahmacharya, a man enters grihastha and thereafter *Vanprastha ashram*. This is the third segment of life which begins after 50 years and goes up to 75 years.

Meaning of Vanprastha

Vanprastha is derived from the Sanskrit word Vanprasth (वानप्रस्थ), which means to live in a forest. This ashram is, therefore, a period of living in a forest. In other words, this is that segment of life, in which a person after completing education and the married life of a householder, leaves his household at the ripe age of 50 or 55 years and above, and spends life in a nearby forest up to the age of 75 years.

Who is a Vanprasthi?

It is clear from the above paras, that one who enters *vanprastha ashram* after completion of grihastha is a Vanprasthi. In ancient days, a householder after crossing the age of fifty years would leave his household and go out to live in a forest. He would either take his wife to live with him or leave her back home to live with his grown-up children. During those days, the population was scarce and towns and cities were less populated and smaller than those at present and forests were also nearby. By the age of 50 years, he would have fully established the household, with grown-up children who are quite capable of shouldering all responsibilities of the household. The father, thus freed from all cares and obligations of the family, could afford to cut off connections with his erstwhile family and leave the household for good.

Spirit of Renunciation

In real sense, entry into *vanprastha ashram* initiates the process of detachment from the worldly material life, which one cherished and adopted while in the *grihastha ashram*. In grihastha, an individual is attached to his house, his wife and children and the profession he follows. He has all sorts of desires which includes sexual, material, emotional etc. and devotes all his time and efforts in fulfilling those desires and aspiration. With the advent of vanprastha, they are left behind, and the sprit of renunciation is awakened, when a vanprasthi lives in the forest far away from his household, village or town where he lived earlier with his family. It is not easy to turn one's back on the alluring comforts of the material world, which is full of all sorts of temptations and material resources. Thus, taking vanprastha is the first step forward on the straight journey of renunciation and detachment, which culminates finally into the final phase of *Sanyasa Ashram*.

At the appropriate time, a *grihastha* who had resolved to enter into vanprastha ashram, would leave his household and go into a nearby forest and start living there in a small hut. While living there, he was completely detached from the city or town life and also free from the worries and anxieties of running a household. This sudden break from the family setup is obviously not easy but is made possible only with the spirit of renunciation, which one has to adopt and practise while living in the forests.

Study and Sadhna in Vanprastha

The final phase of life culminates into Sanyasa, which is extremely difficult. In vanprastha, an individual equips himself with all those necessary qualities which makes him well-equipped and fit for the arduous life of a *sanyasi*. For achieving this, a vanprasthi has to practise and live an austere life of Tapas or Sadhna for which he had to adopt a regimen of hard discipline. Firstly, a vanprasthi has to lead a life of complete celibacy, whether his wife lives with him or away from him. Regular study of scriptures, company of the learned, practice of yogic discipline and moral conduct are the main ingredients of *Sadhna* in vanprastha ashram. He has to live a very simple life, partaking simple and only essential food. He should be kind to all without expecting or accepting anything in return. He need not work extraordinarily hard to secure comforts of living, and keep his desires under full control.

The discipline of vanprastha requires an individual to shun all temptations, desires and attachments which he had gathered around him while living in grihastha ashram. The following verse in the Gita (2:58) is a pointer in this direction:

He who draws away the senses from the objects of the sense on every side as a tortoise draws his limbs.

A vanprasthi has to practise strict discipline of above type for success in this ashrams.

In order to have a life of Tapas or Sadhna, a *vanprasthi* should follow the instructions of Maharishi Manu, quoted below.

'Let him constantly devote himself to studying and teaching, retain a calm mind, be a friend to all, conquer his passion, bestow knowledge upon others and be kind to all living beings. Let him not receive gifts from others. Thus should he conduct himself.'

Maharishi Manu further says:

'Let him not be very solicitous for bodily comfort, let him be a brahmachari, abstain from sexual indulgence, even if his own wife be with him, sleep on the ground, have no inordinate love for his dependents and for his belongings and dwell under a tree.'

Thus *Sadhna*, Study and Selfless conduct are the main practices in *vanprastha ashram,* besides spirit of renunciation and disconnection from worldly relations.

Importance of Vanprastha Ashram

The beginning of vanprastha ashram serves as a dividing line between the two halves of human life. On one side are brahmacharya and grihastha ashrams and on the other are vanprastha and sanyasa ashrams. The two parts of life play different roles but these are stages in the same journey towards the same goal of life. While brahmacharya is the period of preparation for the next stage of life, in the same way, vanprastha is the period of preparation for sanyasa, which is the final stage of life. It is during vanprastha ashram, that an individual matures himself through *Tapas* and *Sadhna* so that he is fully fit to become a *sanyasi*.

Apart from playing an important role in carrying on the journey of spiritual life to its logical end, vanprastha ashram was also an essential means to avoid a vital economic and social problem of unemployment among youth. If existing occupants of different professions are permitted to keep their jobs till death, they will not vacate places for the younger generation, which will thus remain unemployed for want of vacancies. Thus in ancient times, most senior people, after crossing the age of fifty years, would leave their jobs and positions, upon entry into vanprastha ashram and thus make way for the upcoming younger people, who would find ready and timely employment. Thus, there was hardly any problem of unemployment and its connected economic and social evils due to the role played by vanprastha ashram.

The importance of vanprastha ashram may be adjudged from another angle also. Those who entered this ashram were persons of great experience in household affairs and in bringing up children as well as in other social obligations, etc. They had gained sufficient knowledge and experience concerning the growth and development and were also quite aware of the needs of children's emotional, mental and educational planning and progress. After the elders in the family had retired to their forest abodes, the younger people from the nearby village, town etc. would flock to these *vanprasthis* for guidance in the management of family matters, induding business, profession, upbringing of children, etc. Thus, these *vanprasthis* would act as guides and family advisors to the young and inexperienced *grihasthas*.

The *vanprasthis* had a role to play in the field of education of the children. Thus, each *vanprasthi* would run a small educational institution for a number of children from an adjoining village or villages. The children from all strata of society in the neighbourhood received education from the same teacher (called *Guru*) or even from more than one teacher in the same institution or in different institutions called '*gurukuls*'. The education in these *gurukuls* was imparted on basis of equality and without any discrimination. The students of these gurukuls would go to the adjoining village or town to procure free food from the householders who would willingly contribute their share considering this their sacred duty.

The same food, thus procured, was served to all inmates of the ashram. The teachers or gurus in these *ashrams* or *gurukuls* taught free and did not get any salary for doing this work. These *ashrams* or *gurukuls* were run on the basis of financial and material assistance provided by *grihasthis* from nearby villages and towns. All such help was free and on voluntary basis without any compulsion. In this manner, the vanprastha ashram formed the backbone of the educational system of ancient India. Some gurukuls are running in the country even in present time, although in a modified form depending upon the present day requirements. Besides gurukuls for educational purposes of children, there are some other functions also in vanprastha ashrams. Here retired persons who are not happy to live with their grown up children or those who have higher spiritual aspirations but do not find the atmosphere in their household conducive for the same, so they prefer to go to such vanprastha ashram and spend the remaining years of their life in the company of other *vanprasthis*.

Vanprastha ashram, as such, serves dual purpose — one for individual progress on the spiritual path and other for the welfare of the society in the fields of providing education and employment, besides guidance to the younger people. However, the main aim of vanprastha was to prepare an individual for the next ashram of sanyasa. In the vanprastha stage, one would have full opportunity to practise self-control through detachment, study, self-analysis, brahmacharya and yogic discipline.

The transition from the comfortable worldly life of *grihasthi* to the austere, detached forest life is quite difficult. There are instances where some *grihasthis* who had opted for vanprastha, later returned to their households, because they found life in vanprastha very difficult and unacceptable. However, if one remembers the final goal of life and constantly keep it in mind, while marching forward in the journey of life, then the change from grihastha to vanprastha becomes easier and practisable. Similarly, one does not have to remain stuck up in vanprastha.

It has to be remembered that this part of life is also a period of preparation for the next stage, which is sanyasa – the final phase of life constituting the fourth ashram.

The spirit underlying vanprastha ashram is based on the human natural desire for freedom or release from the bondage of mundane life encaged in the extremely busy life of grihastha ashram. While going through the ups and downs of grihastha, and after having enjoyed the temporary and fleeting pleasures of material life — with its attached pains and pit falls – one gets a feeling at some stage, sooner or later, that 'enough is enough' and now is the time to get away from the life of indulgence and extreme involvement in domestic matters and worldly affairs. The human soul yearns for instant or gradual release from the humdrum of grihastha.

In short, vanprastha ashram provides a healthy and scientific opening out of this satiety arising out of human bondage and material attachment.

Special Features of Vanprastha

Renunciation : The spirit of renunciation and detachment forms the basis of vanprastha ashram. Life in a forest, away from human habitation, is solitary and thus more prone to spiritual pursuits, which include meditation and prayer besides contemplation and self analysis, etc.

Freedom From Household : One gets cut off from the household when one enters vanprastha ashram. There are no worries of earning a livelihood, bringing up children and of other domestic chores required for the maintenance of a household. In the forest, all that one needs is a small hut which can be built by his own efforts or with the help of others, who come forward willingly to help a vanprasthi.

***Swadhaya* or Self Study :** As the life in vanprastha is free from domestic obligations, a vanprasthi has ample time at his disposal to study scriptures and other religious literature. In fact, this is the period when he gets plenty of time to attain maturity in philosophical thought and accomplishment of moral values.

Social Welface

A Vanprasthi is a mature person with wide experience of worldly affairs, which he had left behind. He can, therefore, act as a guide to those, who come to receive his help and seek advice for themselves. He can also be a volunteer for providing education to young children from nearby villages. Thus, although free from his family duties, he becomes a source of social welfare.

Stage of Transition

Vanprastha is the third stage of human life and it forms the period of preparation for the fourth and the final phase called sanyasa ashram. It is in this ashram, that one acquires and strengthens all those qualities which prepare a vanprasthi to become a sanyasi – who has no household, no attachments, no material possessions except those essential for the body maintenance. This ashram, therefore, acts as a bridge and a stage of transition from the material to the spiritual domain, where one makes all efforts and sacrifies to attain the final goal of life.

Some Famous Views on Vanprastha

Some of the views expressed by Maharishi Manu on Vanprastha are quoted as follows:

1. 'Having remained in the order of householder, let a twice born man, who had before completed his brahmacharya, live in a forest with his faith firm and his senses well under control.'
2. 'When a householder perceives that his muscles have become flaccid and his hair grey and even his son has become a father, let him then repair to a forest.'
3. 'Let him renounce all the good things of town such as tasty dishes, fine clothes, commit his wife to the care of his sons, or take her with him and dwell in a forest.'
4. Let him discharge his 'Five Great Daily Duties' with various kinds of foods, green herbs, roots, flowers, fruits and tubers and offer the same to *atithis* and himself subsist on the same.'

Maharishi Manu expresses his views on the conduct and way of life in vanprastha, in the following words:

'Learned men of calm minds, living righteous lives in retirement, imbued with the keen desire of knowing and embracing the truth, free from all impurities, subsisting on alms, realise the Unchangeable, Immortal, Omnipresent spirit by the practice of yoga and thereby enjoy true happiness.'

❑❑❑

Sanyas Ashram

'Having passed the third stage of life (i.e. 50 to 75 years) as a vanprasthi in a forest, let a man enter the fourth stage, renouncing all connections and become a Sanyasi.'

[Maharishi Manu]

Sanyas Ashram is the fourth and the last stage of life in the ashram set-up. It is the final phase of life concluding in death and redemption.

The Meaning of Sanyas

In Sanskrit, sanyas is a combination of सम and न्यास, सम means, always the same, unchangeable, uniform, impartial, etc. The meaning of न्यास is to keep away, to renounce, to be detached etc. Thus, sanyas implies a stage of renunciation, detachment, and disconnection from material life.

Who is a Sanyasi

It follows from above, that a sanyasi is one who,

after having renounced all worldly pursuits, leads a detached life and is engaged in spiritual pursuits and study of scriptures. He is also totally involved in the service of mankind in an impartial and selfless manner. The Gita defines a sanyasi as follows:

'He who neither loathes nor desires should be known as one who has ever the spirit of renunciation; free from dualities, is released easily from bondage.'

[Verse 3, Chapter V]

Thus one who is free from dualities and works in a detached spirit is a sanyasi.

The Gita defines a Sanyasi, in another verse, as follows:

'He who does the work which he ought to do without seeking its fruit, he is the sanyasi, he is the Yogi, not he, who does not light the sacred fire and performs no rites.

[Verse 1. Chapter VI]

It is the inward attitude and not the external action which really matters to make a sanyasi.

Who Can Become A Sanyasi?

'Let a man become a Sanyasi on the day he feels free from all worldly cases and affections, no matter whether he is a vanprasthi, a Grihastha or even a Brahmachari.'

[Brahman Granth]

The above verse indicates complete freedom to become sanyasi, at any time but there is a condition attached to it. One has to be free from worldly desires and attachments. However, in the normal course, the following are the three ways of becoming a sanyasi:

1. The first is the consecutive order that has been described before, i.e. by passing through the first three stages successively.
2. The second is that of becoming a sanyasi from grihastha.
3. The third option is that of entering sanyas directly from brahmacharya. This should be resorted to when a man is free from all sensual desires, has attained self-control and knowledge and has an extreme desire to serve the society.

Special Duties of a Sanyasi

The practice of Dharma (righteousness) is obligatory on the part of all orders (Ashrams), that is, for all mankind, but according to Maharishi Manu, the following are the special duties of Sanyasis :

(i) Let him keep his eyes to the ground and never look hither and thither while he walks; let him filter his water before he drinks; let him always speak the truth, and let him think well before he acts, and thus embrace truth and reject falsehood.

(ii) If in the course of a discourse or a discussion a man be angry with him, let him not, in his turn, be angry. Ever though abused, let him say kindly what is good for him; let him never falsify his speech.

(iii) With his soul composed and centred or the supreme spirit, let him be indifferent to pain and pleasure, abstain from meat and intoxicants, seek only spiritual happiness and go about teaching the gospel of truth and enlightening the world with the light of knowledge.

(iv) With his hair, nails, beard and moustache clipped, carrying a suitable water-jar and a staff, wearing ochre-coloured garments, let him go about with a tranquil mind, harming no living being.

(v) Let him restrain his senses from wicked pursuits, renounce affection and hatred, bear no malice to any living creature and work for immortality.

(vi) 'Whether maligned or praised, let a Sanyasi be impartial towards all, practise virtue himself and strive to make others virtuous.

(vii) To elevate the human race by the preaching of truth and the imparting of knowledge and wisdom is the paramount duty of a Sanyasi.

(viii) 'Let a Sanyasi, practise systematically as many Pranayams as he can, meditating on the highest name of God, but let him never practise less than three Pranayams.

Sanyasa – a Privilege of Brahmans

It is said that only Brahmans enjoy the privilege of entering into Sanyasa while others can enter into Brahmacharya and other orders. But here the correct meaning of Brahman should be kept in mind. It does not mean a person born in the so-called Brahman family based on the prevalent obnoxious caste system. The true basis of caste is not birth; it is based on other genuine factors, which include qualities (*guna*), functions performed (*Karma* or action) and intrinsic nature (*swabhav*) . A Brahman is, therefore, a person who is classified as such on the basis of (*guna-karma-swabhav*) i.e. modes, actions and human nature.

Who is a Brahman?

On the basis of the above discussion, let us see who qualifies as a real Brahman. According to the Gita, a brahman should possess and practise following qualities.

'Serenity, self-control, austerity, purity, forbearance, uprightness, wisdom, knowledge and faith in religion.

[VERSE 42. CHAPTER XVIII]

Thus, Brahmans are persons of wisdom and knowledge. Their traits include serenity, self-restraint, purity, austerity, uprightness, forgiveness and righteousness, etc. Such individuals have firm faith in God and moral values. They are righteous people, teachers and spiritual leaders and thus can provide wise counsel and proper guidance to the ruling elite and society in general. It is, therefore, the *Gunas* (traits) which a person possesses, *Karmas* (actions) which he performs in real life and the intrusive nature which determines his attitude – all these make a Brahman and not his birth in a particular family.

One has therefore to fulfil all these conditions before be can become a true *Sanyasi*.

Views On *Sanyasa Ashram*

Some of the famous views on Sanyasa ashram or Sanyasa are mentioned below.

Katha Upanishad

'Let a wise Sanyasi restrain his mind and speech from all that is sinful, and apply them to the acquisition of knowledge and the realisation of his inner self. Let him use his knowledge and then devote his enlightened soul to the realisation of the supreme being and find rest in Him'.

Thus, Sanyasa is a stepping stone to the final goal of life, which is God-realisation. This is the greatest achievement, after which nothing more is left to achieve.

Shatpath Brahman

'Let a Sanyasi renounce all love of fame, love of wealth and power and the enjoyments thereof and love of his kith and kin, live on alms and devote himself day and night to all those things that lead to Eternal Bliss.'

It is clear from the above view, that the life in Sanyasa ashram is hard, without material enjoyments and fully devoted to God.

Bhagwad Gita

We have already quoted a few shlokas as from the Gita, which express views on Sanyasa.

❑❑❑

Ashram Setup and Modern Life

Ashram setup was constituted thousands of years ago when an average human being aspired to live for a hundred years and perhaps even more. The span of life was divided into four equal periods. It was designed to live life in an orderly and planned manner and each life segment had a definite purpose to achieve. Thus Brahmacharya was a period of preparation and it laid the foundation of the whole ashram setup. Without this ashram the very existence of other ashrams was well-nigh impossible or extremely difficult. The next ashram, Grihastha, covered married life and was proper means for the fulfillment of material desires. The third ashram, Vanprastha, initiated a partial withdrawal from mundane life and also started gradual progress on the path of spiritual journey. The last ashram, Sanyasa, formed the last phase of human journey, the end of which was the achievement of the goal of life viz. God-realisation. In ancient times, people generally, followed the ashram set-up and consequently lived a happy, contented, constructive and purposeful life.

Much water has flown since then and the modes of living, surrounding environment, social and material requirements and attitude towards life have undergone a sea change. In olden days human population was far less than it is today. Now it has increased thousands times more. The number of students and young people now has no comparison with that in ancient days. The number of towns, cities and even villages have grown up in larger proportion. The area of forest land has also decreased considerably. The rishis and learned gurus of ancient days are no more visible. The interest towards spiritual matters has diminished considerably. With all these changes and much more, the question arises whether the ashram setup, as prevalent in its original form, is really possible, practicable or even useful in the present day material world, which in view of the tremendous progress and development in science and technology is altogether a new modern world with entirely changed social system and values of life.

As it appears now, the upcoming younger generation has no inkling of the old 'Ashram set-up'. Only the seniors among Hindu families may have traces of remembrance of the old system, in theory but not in practice. Those who actually practise this system may be counted on fingers. The 'Gurukuls' and 'Ashrams' which existed near human habitations in ancient days hardly exist now. The only few ashram and gurukuls which exist now are located in far off places. Some of these have become resting places of retired persons or those abandoned by their children or those who have willingly disconnected themselves from the unhealthy and unbearable environment of their erstwhile households.

The student population has increased to such a large extent that it is impossible to build 'gurukuls' in larger numbers in order to cater to their requirements. The curriculum of school studies, the methods of teaching the variety of subjects to be taught, all these inputs have changed entirely. In these circumstances, it is impossible to enforce the ancient form of ashram setup in the present day modern life.

Notwithstanding what has been stated in the preceding paras, it should be acknowledged that the spirit behind the observance of ashram set-up is valid for all times. It is, therefore, as relevant nowadays as in the ancient times, even though the form in which it has to be practised may be different from what it was in earlier days. The division of lifespan into four segments remains with small variations here and there. Whether we call these segments as 'ashrams' or give some different names dose not make much difference. Our present life is the period between birth and death. An individual marches forward in the journey of life from childhood to youth, then to middle age and retirement and lastly to the final phase, when the life reaches its end. In other words, life consists of growth, youth — which includes married life, retirement and the fag end culminating in death. Thus the four segments of life remain ever, as before and even at present. While in ancient times, these four segments were called as 'Ashrams', we may call them by different names, if some people find objection in having old names. For example, the Brahmacharya Ashram may be seen as the "Foundation' of life. The Grihastha as 'married life' or may even be termed as 'struggle', etc. The third segment or Vanprastha may be viewed as 'life after retirement' from service or a profession and the last segment is the state of advanced age. In the present scenario, the complexion of the last two Ashrams — Vanprastha and Sanyasa, has changed entirely or considerably. We can hardly find any vanprasthis or true sanyasis belonging to the ancient form and tradition.

The very few vanprastha ashrams that exist today do not serve the purpose of ancient ashrams of the same name. These ashrams have become the resting places for the retired people and senior citizens, who can not adjust themselves in the modern homes of their sons and daughter-in-laws. Very few people go there happily and of their own volition. There have been many instances, when some people have gone to live in the ashrams but returned to their old homes soon after because they did not find the environment there congenial and suitable to their expectations. In so far as the last ashram of Sanyasa is concerned, the less said the better it is as very few genuine Sanyasis are visible these days. Those who are roaming in villages and towns, wearing saffron clothes and with begging bowls, are not Sanyasis. Even most of those in similar uniforms who live in Ashrams on rather permanent basis do not practise and fulfil the ideals of true Sanyasa. Some of these may even have a criminal background while some others, fed up with their family's adverse circumstances, might have escaped to these establishments for the sake of convenience.

In view of the changed circumstances as briefly discussed above, while it may not be now practisable to follow ashram setup in the old and traditional form, the spirit behind this setup can be maintained, may be, in a modified form. It is not only desirable but also essential to do so, in order to lead a happy and contented life amidst anxieties and intricacies of present day modern world. Present day human life is full of complexities of pain and pleasures, dreams and despair, indulgence and temptations and varied activities and opportunities. While passing through the complex process of mundane life, an individual acquires material possessions, accumulates wealth and property, gains name and fame, fulfills desires of all sorts and runs after the shadow of happiness. He enjoys temporary pleasures and craves for more and more and thus gets lost in the taste and temptations of material existence. However, a day arrives, sooner or later, when he has to leave all these pleasures and possessions and die. The thought of painful experiences, difficulties and hardships of life makes one ponder about some practical way out of the quicksand of human misery. This is when the need of a useful life support system is felt. Our ancient rishis devised that system in the form of ashram setup, which worked very well then and made human life simple, smooth and happy. The spirit of that very system provides a blueprint for living a good, useful, happy and purposeful life even now in the changed circumstances of modern life. The essence of that system is valid for all times – past, present and future. Let us now discuss how this setup can be made applicable and effective in the modern life of present times.

First Phase : Brahmacharya

Each ashram has a specific purpose for the ongoing journey of human life. The purpose of the first ashram (Brahmacharya) was to lay a strong foundation for the entire structure of life. Its immediate aim was to make an individual fully fit and, competent to lead the next segment of life which is grihastha ashram and, of course, thereafter. The same purpose holds good for modern life. However, the way by which this purpose can be achieved in the changed circumstances of modern age has to be modified to suit the changed environment.

The gurukuls of ancient days do not exist now. Even a few which carry the name of gurukul have changed their complexion. In view of the huge student population, the 'Gurukul' system as was in vogue in ancient days, cannot work now. Modern schools, colleges, universities and other educational institutions have grown up in large numbers to meet the present-day educational requirements. It is therefore essential to teach the present-day school and college going students and young people the basic principles on which the Brahmacharya Ashram rested.

The spirit of celibacy, hard work, moral values, good-health, right education, etc., have to be inculcated among younger generation who enter the portals of educational institutions. This needs to be done simultaneously while imparting general education and professional skills. The fundamentals of celibacy have to be taught and enforced in their minds and life style. The importance of conservation of vital energy and proper sex education has to be indicated to them in a proper and positive manner. The students must be made well-acquainted with the principles, advantages and practices of Brahmacharya. It would be difficult to practise the strict discipline of Brahmacharya unless they fully understand its meaning and importance. This is where both parents and teachers have to play their roles in an effective and useful manner. First of all, parents have to teach their children the basic skills of sitting, standing, walking, speaking, eating, etc. As children grow up at home, they have to be taught fundamentals of good conduct and behaviour and some of the basic moral values like speaking truth, non-violence, non-stealing and non-greed, etc.

The essentials of Brahmacharya include good health and fitness, good character, proper education and complete celibacy in thought, word and deed. These values can be taught both at home and in educational institutions, under the guidance and supervision of both parents and teachers. The spirit of self-discipline and right conduct has to be inculcated from the very beginning, right from home and the same spirit has to be strengthened more and more as the children enter schools and colleges, etc. Proper guidance of parents and teachers is utmost essential during these formative years of life. Habits formed during the first phase of life last longer and greatly influence the subsequent phase, particularly the next phase of grihastha ashram. While bad habits should be curbed with proper education and persuation, good habits should be praised and encouraged.

The modern youth and younger generation are greatly influenced by the modern media which include cinema, T.V. songs, magazines, books and other sources of information, etc. There is a lot of influence of western thought, way of life, mode of education and interaction among people and sexes through media, travel and tourism, etc.

Therefore, regular checks have to be maintained on the activities and engagements of their wards by both parents and teachers. All efforts are required to be put in practice in order to save them from the malpractices and bad influence of any foreign culture. To do this, persuasion and not pressure, peaceful means and not violent methods, and proper education and not ignorant means have to be used in a desirable manner. They should be provided with useful and effective literature which provides useful information about ancient Indian philosophy and culture. Even modern methods through audo-visual aids can be deployed to convey the right message and knowledge so that they imbibe the spirit of those values which are enshrined in brahmacharya ashram.

It is quite evident from the above discussion that while it is impracticable to follow the ancient system of education and mode of bringing up children under the 'gurukul' scheme, it is not only possible but desirable also to promote, practise and encourage the spirit underlying the gurukul system and brahmacharya ashram, while living at home and studying in school and colleges. What is really needed is the proper environment and useful guidance.

Second Phase: Married Life

The second phase of life consists of Grihastha Ashram which was considered the greatest ashram in ancient days. It constitutes the life of a householder which includes married life and its requirements, obligations and duties, etc., which we have already discussed in detail earlier.

In spite of modern age and its modifications, this phase of life still remains the most important. In changed circumstances, there is great emphasis on the economic aspect. This is the period of life when an individual puts all his efforts to acquire economic prosperity. He has to earn his livelihood to maintain a household, to raise a family, to educate children, to enjoy pleasure of life and to fulfil various types of worldly desires, etc.

All the requirements of this ashram still remain but there is a big difference. Firstly, modern marriage has become a very costly affair with all the pomp and show and the false sense of pride, which reflects in the manner in which modern day marriages are being celebrated. Marriage which was considered a sacred bond and a duty to lead a purposeful life, has become a source of sexual gratification and a great means of fulfillment of mundane desires which make people go astray from the real goal of life. Evils like lust, greed, anger and violence and several other undesirable practices like dowry, child marriages, incompatible and unholy alliances have crept in to a large extent. In order to lead a peaceful, happy and purposeful life, all these evils have to be curbed from the current marriage system. Let us examine how this can be done in the modern age.

First of all, the real significance of marriage has to be understood by the young persons, who are going to enter into wedlock. This can be done by their own individual efforts, by reading useful literature or through proper counselling of wise, educated and truly religious persons who are well aware of our ancient culture and traditions. Of course, parents and other elderly people in the family can provide essential guidance to their grownup children regarding sexual relations, the purpose of marriage, etc., on the basis of their study and personal experiences. Proper sex education should be available in colleges and universities etc., besides homes. In short, marriage should not to treated as a free license for limitless sexual gratification and a means of pleasure. What is needed is proper regulation of sexual indulgence, family planning and family welfare. The concept and content of marriage as a sacred bond of love between the individuals and a means to promote the purpose of God through a pure and desirable act of procreation has to be made clear to the marrying couples. Due to ignorance of the real purpose of marriage, numerous cases of divorce, failure of marriage, dowry deaths, suicides, cases of violence and torture, besides maltreatment of women and other abuses and ailments have become everyday news in the present age. Marriages are also being performed on commercial lines and lakhs of rupees are being spent and wasted in unnecessary rituals, festivities and ostentatious decorations and pandals, etc. All these malpractices should be avoided and the same money can be spent to serve some noble cause of providing financial help to the deserving, needy, poor, helpless, sick, disabled members of society.

It is, therefore, utmost essential to highlight the real significance of married life and hence of this segment (ashram) of life.

The second most important aspect of this part of life is related with economic well-being. In ancient days life was very simple, needs and desires were very limited and therefore, the urge to earn money was kept within desirable limits. This scenario has undergone a drastic change in view of the modern scientific and technological developments, which are ever increasing and seen to have no limits. The avenues of leading a luxurious, comfortable, pleasant and endless material life with grandeur and goodies have expanded considerably. Consequently, the ever increasing greed to have 'more and more' money, to have 'more and more' material possessions has become rampant everywhere. It may be relevant to quote Mahatma Gandhi, as follows :

> *'The world has everything to fulfil all*
> *men's needs but not one man's greeds.'*

In the married life, a proper check has to be put on greed. As there is no end to greed the fulfillment of desires of married life and other mundane desires are required to be kept within a certain limit. The means of livelihood have to be honest, pure and proper and without greed.

We have already mentioned earlier that all other ashrams in ancient days, by and large, owed their existence and substance upon 'grihastha ashram.' The people in this ashram provided financial and other material help to the incumbents of other three ashrams. Similarly in the present age also, it is the people who belong to this part of life (married households) who play the greatest role in the social and economic well-being of the society in which they live. Thus, most professionals, which include businessmen, doctors, lawyers, teachers, government servants and other people who work in some other spheres of public and private life are married householders. All of them have great role, to play in the progress and development of society and the country as a whole. Most of them pay taxes to the government, are part of administrative and other professional setups and thus are serving the various sections of society in some form or the other. There are others who run charitable organisations and thus help the needy, poor, underprivileged, handicapped and other similar people who are in need of financial and material help.

We have already covered various aspects of grihastha ashram in greater detail as prevalent in ancient times. The spirit of grihastha ashram should continue to prevail. In the present age, there would be one obvious difference from the olden times.

In those days, a *grihastha* had a fixed abode. However, in the present times, an individual may change residences, localities, places and even villages, towns or a city depending upon his increasing needs, desires and requirements. In case of government servants, they have to change places in view of their frequent transfers. But the basic condition remains the same as he has to establish a household wherever he goes.

While there is scope for sexual indulgence in this part of life, the spirit of scope of Brahmacharya should prevail to a reasonable extent. In other words, sexual relations with one's wife have to be well-regulated in order to maintain good health of both the partners. While this segment of life has to be utilised for fulfillment of desires, economic well-being, management of household affairs, procreations, material progress and achievements, it is essential that all these have to be done within appropriate limits. The motto should be 'Self-restraint Vs self-indulgence'. All sensual and material pleasures and enjoyments should be kept under desirable checks and restraints. This is to ensure that after due fulfillment of duties and obligations of this period of life, an individual is fully prepared to leave his household and to shift to the next segment of life which involves considerable withdrawal from the material world.

Third Phase: Vanprastha

The third segment of life, which was in ancient times known as Vanprastha, may be compared now with the life of retirement from service or job or some other form of active life of a householder. By this time, an individual might have completed most or all of his domestic obligations and responsibilities arising out of married life of a householder. His children have grown up, got educated and married and well-settled in some profession or some other work and they are no longer dependant upon their father or parents, as they used to be earlier. At this stage, the householder of older days, who was the manager of the show then, seems to have become rather redundant and lonely. A similar situation arises even now, sooner or later after retirement, when the present age householder gets older, less active and feels himself rather a burden on the family. He is no longer an active service provider, may have no source of any personal income and his health may have also deteriorated and is not at all in a commanding position in the family as his children have become adults and taken his place. He must, therefore, withdraw himself from active worldly life and inculcate an attitude of detachment. He need not go to a forest or any other place as it may not be feasible to do so because of deterioration in health or for want of financial resources. He should continue to live in the same house as he needs proper care and assistance from the members of his family.

In an ideal situation even now it is better, at this stage, to seek a better haven outside their previous home to which they were immensely attached. Such a willing and purposeful withdrawal from their home should be good for them as well as their grownup children. But this could be possible only in a very few cases where the concerned persons are in a state of good physical and financial health. But, in general, the elders nowadays are not in a fit position to live independently outside their homes as they require proper care and assistance from others and the same can be provided by their young children. The best course, in present circumstances, would be to bring about a change in their mental attitude. They should, therefore, continue to live with their children, adopting an appropriate and respectable course of close cooperation and mutual adjustment in a willing, happy and cheerful manner. Of course, such an attitude should prevail on both sides – children as well as parents but the latter have to make more efforts and adjustment in the modern day changing environment. It is, however, very desirable that their young sons and daughters-in-law should reciprocate in a positive manner and treat their elders with love and respect. However, if this is not at all possible then, perhaps, the only alternative is to withdraw to some old-age home or *Vanprastha Ashram* run by some well meaning, charitable, religious organisation, etc. Otherwise the elderly people will have no option but to lead a miserable life with their unwilling and uncooperative kith and kin, as is happening in several unfortunate cases nowadays.

In short, what is essential is to carry on with other members of family, to think and behave with a spirit of detachment and non interference. One should try to do what is physically possible for the welfare of the family and also for the welfare of the society, in general. It is useful to chalk out some daily schedule. For example, one can go for walk outside, meet other elderly people in some public park, join some welfare charitable society and association and help them in their social work. It would also be beneficial to attend some religious gatherings in a temple or other religious places where one can listen to spiritual discourses and exchange views with other persons of the same age group. Reading of good literature is another useful activity which one can carry on to make better use of spare time. One can also help younger children in their studies, etc. It would be a source of great pleasure to play and laugh with infants, who are a great source of joy and happiness. Thus, the retired person can find several ways to utilise his time in useful and pleasant pursuits. Personal involvement in such constructive activities will be a source of pleasure not only for him but also for others around him. In this way, one can put a sparkle of joy in, otherwise, a gloomy old age.

The Final Phase: Sanyasa

In the present state of circumstances, the last segment of life has become very difficult, barring some exceptions of a few fortunate persons who are blessed with good health and the company of loving and respectful close relatives and companions. In present times, most people who reach this stage (75–100) are not fit enough to take Sanyas in the old form as they cannot undergo the rigours and face the hard situations of this ashram, which involves continuous travel without any financial means and material support. As such, elderly people in this stage of life have no option but to continue staying with their families, as in the earlier stage. Most of such persons may be suffering from some ailment and, therefore, would require regular medical treatment and constant care of their family members. The lucky few may get good care and pass the final phase of their life in good affectionate environment of love and respect and then gradually fade away peacefully.

There is another situation when a ditermined and detached person leaves home to face all strange, rough and tough situations.

As taking Sanyas in the real sense, as in ancient times, is not possible in the present age (except in rare cases) the best course is to assume and practise an attitude of Sanyas. The desires and daily personal needs must be willingly cut down to the bare minimum and much time should be spent in meditation and other spiritual pursuits like study of scriptures and spread of spiritual knowledge among others, in whatever way possible. One can deliver discourses on spiritual topics or write some books, etc. It may be worthwhile to join some charitable society to do some social service, if it is physically possible.

We have already discussed in some detail, the duties and requirements of Sanyasa Ashram in an earlier chapter. All those things may not be possible in the present age for most individuals. What is needed in present changed circumstances, is the mental attitude which can be cultivated through the sprit of genuine detachment, true faith in God and constant meditation.

In conclusion, while it may not be completely practisable to regulate the journey of life in accordance with the requirements of ancient form of Ashram setup in the present day changed environment, the main principles on which this social system was based can be followed in spirit, if not in letter.

First of all, the spirit of 'Brahmacharya' which forms the foundation of human life should be given due consideration and practised as far as possible, in all phases of existence. As old gurukuls do not exist now, the present-day younger generation has to go to the community schools and colleges where the environment is entirely different from old ashrams and gurukuls. However, they must be given proper guidance and instructions about the basic requirements of brahmacharya, both by parents and teachers. Parents should assume greater responsibility in this regard so that their wards do not go astray, fall in bad company or acquire evil practices and habits which may later ruin their life and career.

The present-day householder must understand the meaning and purpose of married life and therefore should fulfil his duties and responsibilities in an appropriate manner and within desirable moral constraints. He must also ensure that he completes his domestic obligations well in time so that at an appropriate age, he becomes free from his responsibilities, becomes detached as and when his grown up children are fit and ready to take on all responsibilities of the household. In brief, the purpose and the ways of proper performance of journey of all, through all its four segments, must be well understood in the light of teachings and instruction left by our ancient rishis and guides.

It is not necessary that we, in the present age, stick to the old form as it is not possible to do so. What really matters is the spirit and the true significance underlying the ashram setup, and the same has to the carried forward, making necessary modifications wherever necessary, keeping the main principles unaltered. Human life should be lived in such a manner that its one segment gradually and smoothly leads to the next, after one has performed suitably all obligations of the preceding segment; passing through its pains and pleasures, duties and responsibilities, etc., in a natural and orderly manner.

The purpose of human life must be kept in view and if the main principles and percepts of the Ashram setup are understood and followed properly, it may not be inpossible to attain the final goal of life.

❑❑❑

In a Nutshell

In the preceding chapters, we have described in some detail various ingredients of Ashram Setup, which was devised by our rishis to live life in a planned and purposeful manner. This was indeed a Master Plan for human life. This social setup worked very well in ancient times. In view of changed circumstances, most of the old traditions and practices may not be practisable now. However, the basic philosophy underlying this setup is valid for all times. Therefore it should be continued even in modern times with appropriate modifications, as mentioned in the previous chapter. We may now recapitulate briefly what has been already discussed earlier, so that the reader can easily remember the basic principle of this system, at a glance.

Bhahmacharya

It lays down the very foundation of human life and is meant to be a period of necessary preparation for the whole life. An individual is supposed to acquire good health, essential education, good character, moral values besides professional skill to earn a living. One is required to observe complete celibacy in this period of life. There is no scope for sexual indulgence in any form, whether in thought, word or deed. The immediate aim of this ashram is to make an individual fit and capable to enter the next segment – which is Grihastha, and enable him to fulfil its duties, responsibilities and desires in a proper and successful manner.

Grihastha

It is the middle part of life and the most important in as much as an individual gets married, establishes a household, raises his family and follows a profession to earn his livelihood. It is in this ashram, that one fulfills worldly desires of acquiring wealth, children, material possessions and earn name and fame. This is a period of great struggle amid pleasures and pains of material life. It should be noted that while sexual gratification is permitted in this ashram, its chief aim is procreation, and enjoyment of sexual pleasure should be kept within appropriate constraints. All norms of personal and social conduct are required to be maintained as far as possible.

Vanprastha

This is a period of withdrawal from the worldly life of a householder. One should retire from active professional life and entrust responsibilities of running the household to the grownup children. It is not necessary to leave the household and retire to the forest, as required in ancient times. What is required, is a change in the mental attitude and withdrawal from the active association and attachment to the activities of the household. However, one may continue giving guidance to the younger generation, wherever and whenever required. While keeping limited contacts, one should avoid unnecessary interference in the life of other members of the family maintaining a posture of positive aloofness. One can take part in some social service outside the home and devote much time towards study of good literature, meditation and other spiritual pursuits of listening to spiritual discourses and discussions, etc. It may be kept in view that this is a period of preparation for the final phase of life, which involves complete withdrawal from the mundane activities. Vanprastha, therefore, is a stepping stone towards sanyasa. It is in this period that one makes necessary preparation and acquires necessary qualifications which enable him to enter the final phase of life.

Sanyasa

This is the last segment and the final phase of life. It involves an extremely difficult discipline which is not easy to follow by most individuals. Only person of rare calibre and necessary qualifications can become *Sanyasis*. In an ideal situation, one is required to disconnect from all relations with the earlier household, the family and also the obligations of the material world. However in present times, for most people it may not be possible to leave the household due to various compulsions. One should therefore remain in home and cut down desires and needs to the minimum and spend time in the study of scriptures, other good literature and in the company of learned people of similar age and situation. Prayer and meditation are the main engagements of this part of life. If possible, one can utilise sometime in instructing others about spiritual matters. The final phase of life, therefore, should be lived with a spirit of detachment, even-mindedness and thinking of God always — with full devotion, purity of mind and sincerity. Following the discipline, one many exit from this world in a state of bliss and contentment.

In conclusion, the Ashram Setup is a Master Plan to live life in four stages. The first stage is that of preparation to acquire suitable knowledge and skills, necessary physical strength and mental capability, moral values and principles of good conduct. The middle stage of life is meant for worldly pursuits involving pleasures and pains and fulfillment of mundane desires. The next stage requires withdrawal from the worldly life in order to prepare for the final stage of non-attachment, self-control and spiritual perfection, leading to a peaceful exit from the world.

The Ashram set-up was devised keeping in view the final goal of God-realisation. Human life was divided into four segments in such a way that one part leads smoothly to the other, as an individual advances in age and leads to the final goal. This is indeed an ideal time-table to live life, following which, an individual can achieve all accomplishments (Material, Moral, and Spiritual) of life in a smooth, sustained and successful manner.

The End

The real purpose of our existence is not to make a living only, but to make a life. And it can be made through proper planning.

There is no plan for life better than the Master plan, which lies in Ashram setup. There are four stages of life : Birth, development, decline and destruction. There are also Four Ashrams. Life is also a journey from imperfection to perfection. This journey can be best traversed through four Ashrams.

So follow this master plan of life to attain perfection.

❑❑❑